Lan

LAN ANH HOÀNG

Copyright © 2024 Lan Anh Hoàng

The right of Lan Anh Hoang to be identified as the Author of the Work has been asserted by her in accordance with the Copyright, Designs and Patents Act, 1988.

All rights reserved.

The first ever picture of me – taken when I was around 15 years of age. I paid about 3,000 đồng for it (about 11 pence now), and this included the hire of the smart clothes, shoes, make-up and, of course, the tennis racket.

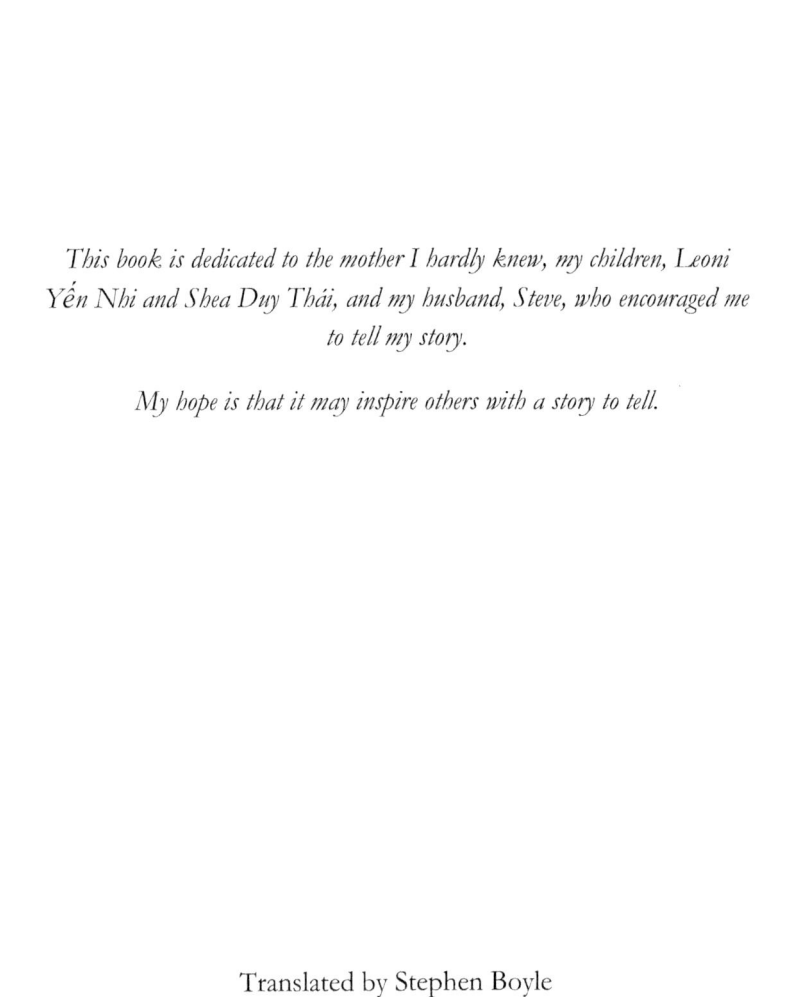

This book is dedicated to the mother I hardly knew, my children, Leoni Yến Nhi and Shea Duy Thái, and my husband, Steve, who encouraged me to tell my story.

My hope is that it may inspire others with a story to tell.

Translated by Stephen Boyle

Lan

The green banana

I am seven years old, or thereabouts. Our neighbours, who are even poorer than we are, have eight children. That makes ten mouths to feed. Even though they are distant cousins my father always has a problem with them. Like us they live in a simple, one-room hut with a tatty thatch roof and walls made of compacted mud and hay. But their hut is even scruffier than ours, and we seem to have more provisions, such as our pile of unhusked rice. My father always waits until the price is good before selling this, no matter how hungry we are, to buy fertiliser for our fields. Much of it he keeps to make rice wine. He never sells that. My neighbours don't seem to have the option of storing food. They live hand-to-mouth. If they have some food they eat it there and then. No waiting.

But I dream of the life they lead. Such freedoms they have – the younger children don't even have to go out to work. That is done by the parents and older siblings. And I notice that they work together as a team: each seems happy to join in. The youngest children stay at home and play, or roam around without anybody keeping an eye on them. As I watch them play, I have steam coming from my ears such is my workload. Depending on the season this could be planting or harvesting rice or sweet potatoes; it could be weeding our vegetable plot; but often it would be foraging for food – for us or for our pigs, chickens or ducks. It could also be wading through paddy fields looking for creatures to eat. I hated this job most of all because it meant I might pick up another leech, or even come into contact with a snake.

I'd already been bitten once. It was while I was searching for creatures to eat – mainly little land crabs, or snails, shrimps or small fish that would hide in hollows in the paddy-field banks. I would blindly have to put my hand into each hollow and feel around for anything that moved. On this occasion I slid my hand into a hollow, and the creature inside sunk its teeth into my finger. I recoiled in shock and jumped out of the water. I could see the snake's teeth marks in my finger. I was terrified as I didn't know if the snake was poisonous. But the fear of my father was greater, and I knew that I couldn't return home empty-handed.

A villager passing by stopped when he saw my distress. I explained what had happened and he said that normally snakes that lived in the water were not poisonous, so I would probably be okay. His words reassured me enough to go back into the paddy water – although not enough for me to plunge my hands blindly into another hollow. I returned home that day with only snails – the one creature you could find without having to rummage around the paddy banks.

We had more land to farm and fewer hands to work it than our neighbours. But although we had a lot more than they did, unlike their children we were constantly hungry. Our father controlled our food supplies with an iron fist. We children had only scraps to eat – much of it foraged. We would never buy food from the market.

As my father only really delegated work, barking out orders through the day, there was always something I had to do, and we were always working on empty stomachs. Regularly, I would watch my neighbours' children as they pulled morsels of food from their pockets. They would have snatched it while their parents weren't looking, of course. Out of their pockets would come pieces of pork or chicken, which they would slowly chew or lick – making sure that every child watching knew they had meat to eat. Meat was such a luxury in those days. I would stand there drooling, literally – not quite believing their luck.

Sometimes, when the weather was poor and the family couldn't go to forage, the neighbours would boil a big pot of water and cook some green bananas, plucked from the few trees they had in their garden. I remember watching this process – and wondering how the green bananas, once cooked, changed colour to a dark grey. Such alchemy. Once cooked, the bananas would be tipped into a large, bamboo colander to drain the water, and the contents would be casually dropped into a pile in front of their hut. There seemed to be hundreds of bananas steaming in those piles.

One day I noticed that their pot was boiling and the green bananas had been picked, ready to be cooked. I decided to try my luck. I waited for the colander to appear and the pot to be drained before casually making my move – walking past their hut hoping that they might notice and spare me one. I stared at the pile of steaming fruit as I walked along, but nobody called me over. So I turned on my bare heels and walked slowly back, hoping that they might yet notice me. This time my luck changed as one of the children called to me: "oi!" I skipped over to an outstretched hand holding a cooked banana. Not quite believing my luck I quickly looked left and right to check that my father wasn't watching. Had he have been I would have been in big trouble. He hated the neighbours. But at the last second fear gripped me at the potential consequences and as I approached the fruit I stopped, looked down and shook my head. I realised that had I have accepted the gift and my father found out we would both have had a big problem, not just me. That didn't seem fair, so I walked away. Still hungry.

Our garden had at least 100 banana trees, but never once had the thought entered my head that even one banana could be boiled to produce something so delicious-looking. Had any of us have done so we would have been severely beaten. Our bananas were there to sell, not to be eaten.

If you've never seen one growing, a banana bunch of the variety we grew has fruit of cascading sizes from the top to the bottom. At the very bottom will often be a few tiny fruits – so small that they can't be sold. One particularly hot day, while my father was asleep, I went into the garden to cool down – under the shade of a banana tree. Looking up, I noticed that a bunch above me had some of the tiny, green fruit. This time I reached up and tried to pluck some. It was tough to tease them away from the stem, but eventually I managed it. With an aching thumb I quickly peeled my ill-gotten gains to uncover the tiny bit of fruit that lay within. I was terrified of my father waking, so I gobbled down the bitter-tasting flesh of the green bananas as quickly as I could. The juice from the fruit made my thumb turn black.

I heard my father call: "Lan ơi!" and a chill ran through me. I was sunk. I walked over and he looked at me and shouted: "Ăn gì đấy?" (what have you eaten?). I was terrified, and quickly denied that I had eaten anything. But he was furious and said that I had to tell him the truth. I knew I was in trouble so decided to tell him that I had eaten some guava buds, which had absolutely no value and were one of the few things in the garden I was allowed to eat without asking. That seemed to satisfy him, so I quickly slid away, my lips – I later discovered – black with the stain of banana juice. It was lucky he hadn't noticed.

My story

My name is Lan Anh Hoàng and now I have a good life. I have two children and a husband who care for me, as I care for them. I live in a small town in Kent in the UK. It's good here – people are generally kind and polite; the land is green and fertile. But there's something missing from my life. I have a half-sister and she disappeared when she was no more than nine months old. She was born in my home village in northern Việt Nam, but we had to leave there to work for distant relatives of my stepmother's. They lived in Yên Bái, a poor mountainous province in the country's north. I was 11 years old, or thereabouts – my birth date hadn't been properly registered. My sister's name is Luyến.

The tap

We left our village out of desperation. January wasn't a growing season and that year we hadn't enough supplies from the last harvest to see us through to the springtime. Although we had a few chickens left they were there to be sold, our staples were virtually gone, and we were reduced to relying on the tiny freshwater crabs and snails to eat, or other scraps of food we could forage or scavenge from the paddy fields. This was a particularly cold winter and the water we waded through would bite. But we had no choice as foraging was the best chance we had of eating any protein. As well as wild foods this included scavenging for anything left behind or discarded by farmers. Our staple in such times was sweet potato – although rarely the variety that was considered best for cooking. Our sweet potatoes were the scrappy lumps that farmers tossed aside – considered by most people to be too small to bother with – or, even worse, of the tasteless variety that was grown locally as pig food. We would boil whatever sweet potatoes we had in a big

The only picture of my mother in existence – captured from the tiny, and very grainy, picture on her ID card (left).

My father as a young man, aged around 20 years old, taken from his ID card (right).

pot and eat them straight from the colander[1], sometimes along with the uppermost leaves from the plant, which were edible but also without taste – and, worse, were covered in fine hairs. Although this was at least some food, the monotony of this diet was hard to bear. I dreaded those starchy, flavourless potatoes and leaves.

Being old enough to look after an infant, but deemed too young to properly work, I had been chosen to travel with my stepmother – to look after my baby sister while my stepmother worked. I had three younger sisters: Ly, Liễu and Luyến. Ly, the eldest of the three, was eight or nine years younger than me, which would have made her about three years of age, with Liễu

---

[1] At this time sweet potatoes were for many people the staple crop during certain months of the year – especially for those families whose rice stores were insufficient to keep them until the next rice harvest. Unlike today, with higher-yield rice, there were only two rice harvests a year in the north compared with three today.

about two and Luyến about five months old. My elder siblings were Liên, who was one year older than me, and our brother, Long, who would have been 13 at the time[2]. People would call out: "con mèo tha con chuột!" (the kitten drags the mice) when they saw me walking around our village with my siblings dangling from my hips.

Although I was older than they were I was small and scrawny for my age. We were always dressed in rags, and our stomachs were distended through lack of food. Ironic, really, that we looked so full. Our meagre diet was supplemented by stolen grains of unhusked rice from our supplies, or maybe a raw sweet potato – eaten while foraging. Anything I could scavenge or take when my father wasn't looking. But now I was leaving this village life. My stepmother, Mợ Hà (Stepmother Ha), hoped to work for her distant relatives on their land in the mountains. Things had to be better there.

The night before we left we had a small ceremony in our hut – to ask for our ancestors' help with our mission. My father did the rarest of things – killing one of our last chickens to cook, along with some rice and noodles. Once cooked, each dish was placed on the little altars to our ancestors. Every home in Việt Nam, no matter how big or small, or rich or poor, must have an altar for such offerings.

Our hut had two altars – one for the ancestors of my father, and one for my mother, who had died when I was just three years

---

[2] As was typical in rural Việt Nam, siblings were often separated by about one year, where the parents remained together.

old. She had grabbed hold of a live electricity cable that had fallen on to a field that we owned[3].

As the incense burned, we each stood in front of the altars to say a prayer. As is usual, once the incense sticks had burned through about halfway, my father took down the food after offering his prayers. The food had been divided between each altar. First, he took down the food from his ancestors' altar. But as he reached up to take the food from my mother's altar it slipped and fell to the dirt floor below. I looked up and saw that my father was closely examining the chicken's feet. He took a sip of his rice wine and looked at us with red eyes, saying; "không tốt! không tốt!" (not good, not good). On the few occasions he would cook one of our chickens, my father would always look at the alignment of the bird's feet when the meat was cold. He believed that he could see his fortune depending on how the feet had distorted during cooking. The omens from this bird were clearly not good.

The journey to the mountains was long and arduous. I can remember clambering on to buses that were bulging with people and their goods – mostly heading to market. Buses in those days were used to haul anything from bicycles to chickens and pigs, which would be trussed up and hauled on to the roof before being strapped down as they screeched their disapproval. There were several bus journeys that day and once we had jumped from the last of the buses we had to walk for many kilometres along dusty tracks before we reached the relatives' house.

---

[3] In those days, the electricity supply was intermittent. On this day, my mother would probably have thought that the power was off, as it normally was, and presumed that the cable wasn't live. She was 29 years of age.

When we arrived at their home it was clear that we weren't welcome. Our visit was unannounced and, to make matters worse, they had no blood connection to me, which meant I had no business being there. I was made to feel this from the off.

On our first day my stepmother, Mợ Hà, went with the rest of the adults to work in the fields. While they were out the family's children taunted and picked on me, and when their parents returned told them that I had been tormenting them. After just a few days Mợ Hà told me we had to leave, and leave immediately. It seemed to me that the lies their children had told about me had worked. There was no argument to be had. It was already night time and pitch black, the air punctuated by the sound of cicadas. There were no lights, just some faint moonlight as we stumbled away from their house. We walked and walked. Other than the insects I heard only the muttered prayers of my stepmother – calling on the spirits of our ancestors to protect us from harm.

I didn't know what to do. All I knew is that I had to follow her. I was scared. I knew we had been thrown out of the house and couldn't return, but also knew that she would be beaten terribly by my father if we returned to our village with nothing. I later found out we had supposed to have been gone for at least three months, to return with either money or foodstuffs – most likely cassava root – or both, in time to work in the new planting season.

The light of the fireflies terrified me. I believed they were the spirits of the dead as they danced around us. The hairs on the back of my neck stood on end. We walked through the night and near daybreak, as the mountains that surrounded us emerged slowly from the darkness, we stumbled by chance upon a railway line. We followed the line until we found a small station. There was nobody there – just a few seats outside. I was exhausted and fell asleep straight away. Eventually the first train of the morning arrived and my stepmother hauled me and little Luyến on to it, and I listened as she begged the guard to not throw us off. We had no idea where the train was heading. It was enough to know it was going somewhere. The guard must have taken pity on her, and once she knew we were safe on the train Mợ Hà started to beg for food from the passengers. She was given a few scraps and, after eating my share, I fell asleep.

Eventually I awoke and as the train rumbled along the countryside started to give way to roads and houses, and then we passed through slow, winding sections where people lived crammed into tiny rooms and apartments that were so close to the train you could almost reach out and touch them. I gazed out of the window at these unfamiliar scenes – of people cooking, laundry drying, children playing and scurrying around as the train trundled slowly past. By chance, we had arrived in Hà Nội.

We had nothing but the clothes we were wearing. We didn't even have ID, which in those days as now made us vulnerable. My stepmother's only option was to beg for money or food, in fact anything at all – even clothes as ours were just rags.

Not far from the station were some public toilets with a tap on the wall outside and a rubbish tip on some neighbouring rough land. It may not have looked much but to us it meant that we at least had access to a water supply and, with the rubbish, the possibility of finding some scraps to eat. Mợ Hà must have quickly decided that the three of us could survive in this new location – at least for now – by scavenging and begging, and sleeping rough. The fact was, anything was better than having to face the wrath of my father. The rubbish tip was our lifeline. We would sift through the waste searching for anything even remotely edible – sometimes there would be bits of fruit or vegetables that we could wash in the tap water before eating.

The public toilets were a valuable resource for others on the margins. On the first morning I watched as a farmer from an outlying village came to collect the human waste from the toilets – in barrels strapped to the back of his bicycle. He must have been later than usual because a stallholder berated him for pushing his stinking bicycle past her customers as they ate.

After a few weeks we had begged enough money to buy a kettle, and – together with a few bricks and some paper and sticks we had scavenged from the rubbish tip – we could now cook any food that we found. Each day I was sent to the nearby market (Ngo Sỹ Liên) to scavenge for any bits that had dropped from stallholders' baskets. They all thought I was a thief and would quickly shoo me away. But I had no option but to persist, and would hover around no matter what they did. On a good day it would be dry and the few nuts or pulses that fell would land on dry ground and be easy to pick up; on a bad day it was wet and the ground muddy. I would have to sift through the mud to pull out the grains and wash them under the tap when I returned.

When we cooked it was against the wall of the station – and we always had be careful not to annoy anybody, especially those who worked there. We were the new bụi đời (literally the 'dust of life') on the scene and, as there were already people living rough there, we had to be especially careful. We would always move on if told to do so – especially by those with some stake in the area. Living rough on the streets made you extremely vulnerable – you had no status, no right to be there, no right to question anybody who told you what to do. To make matters worse, there was always a street hierarchy in such areas based on intimidation and violence, or the threat of it.

The hoodlums who ran things were known as đầu gấu (literally, 'bear heads'). They would start as small-time criminals, often pickpockets, always on the lookout for easy pickings from the vulnerable. If they were particularly vicious they would start to claim territories as their reputations spread. I quickly learned whose gazes to avoid. Generally though, we were so conspicuously the poorest of the poor that we escaped their attentions. At least in the beginning.

As time went by we had enough money to buy some provisions to sell and we watched carefully how other people went about this. My stepmother bought two small bowls, some fresh green tea leaves (from Yên Bái) and, filling our kettle from the tap, we started to sell tea. Many people did the same – selling to market traders or travellers.

Our set-up wasn't tea for the smartly dressed travellers though, we looked too dirty and scruffy for that, but it was at least quick and cheap and we would bring it to traders or poorer travellers for their convenience.

The best thing about living near the station was that at night we could sleep in the main entrance hall. It had great ceiling fans and we would put our mats down on the floor to sleep after paying a few hào[4] for the night. Having a fan overhead was my greatest luxury.

As hard as life was it was still an improvement on the life we had left. In the village we worked constantly and always lived in fear of my father's temper, and hunger. Here, we had a roof to sleep under, some simple food to eat and no beatings. I was happy with things at the station.

I quickly began to familiarize myself with goings on in the area. When you are as vulnerable as we were it is vital to your survival that you observe carefully what is going on around you at all times – especially who the dangerous people are, and any opportunity that may arise to find something of value, such as food to eat. I learned quickly. An early lesson was how to tell how comfortably off or otherwise people were. This was an easy lesson to learn. The well-to-do were those who could afford to walk in plastic sandals; the poor had bare feet. Of course when the sandals were worn by travellers, this marked wearers out as potential targets for the station thieves. Even their sandals were vulnerable.

With no seats to sit on, people would often take off one sandal to sit on, with their bare foot balanced on their other foot as they squatted down. Better than sitting on the dusty floor. But without realising it their every action was being monitored closely, and as soon as they stood up a child would pounce – quickly snatching the single sandal from behind them, leaving the bemused victim to puzzle where the sandal was when seconds earlier they had been sat on it. I'd hear the call 'nhanh

---

[4] There were 10 hào to a đồng, so this was very little money.

như ăn cắp' (as fast as a thief). Life was such a struggle in those days that anything that could potentially be sold was vulnerable to theft, even single plastic sandals.

Our new life of relative security was short-lived – just a few months. One day I sold a cup of tea to a lady who was a long-time trader at the market. She sold live chickens. As usual I was carrying the kettle and walking around calling out "ai trà nóng đây?" (who wants hot tea?). But the trader spat the tea out and screeched that it wasn't hot enough. I didn't know what to do as she hadn't paid me, so I went to Mợ Hà to tell her and she went to have words with the trader. But an argument followed that quickly turned into a fight. Mợ Hà was beaten and the trader ripped all of her clothes in the process. People crowded around to watch and eventually my beaten stepmother said we had to go. She held my baby sister close in an effort to cover her bare skin and walked around in a terribly agitated state. Without clothes to wear our already precarious state was simply impossible. Mợ Hà must have known this and in her state of torment she made a terrible decision – one that I have spent my life regretting: she said that there was no alternative but to sell one of us. She knew that little Luyến was the biggest burden she faced, and called out that she would sell her for 2,000 đồng (worth about 7 pence now).

I can't remember how much time passed, but eventually a man came along who seemed interested in buying my sister. A price was agreed and bystanders told Mợ Hà that she needed to go to the nearby police station (opposite the train station entrance) to complete registration papers so that when the baby was older she would at least know who her real family was. When we arrived at the police station Mợ Hà was interrogated by the police on duty – they were asking her for personal details of Luyến and herself. But she replied to hardly any questions – giving only her own name and that of my sister, and her age. She was clearly too scared to give them my father's name and address for fear of what he would do if he found out. The police said that without my father's details and village address they could not provide any paperwork. There would be no record of who her family was.

We left the police station and I could only watch as Mợ Hà marched quickly away. The man who was interested in buying my sister followed her, along with a few people from the crowd. After some time some people returned and told me that my sister had "gone with a cyclo driver". I was struck with fear and frantically ran to find Mợ Hà to check if this was true. When I found her I saw that my sister was not in her arms. I called out after her "em ơi!" (little sister!), but of course my calls were unanswered. She was gone. Mợ Hà said nothing.

When others asked what she was going to do with me Mợ Hà said she was planning to sell me as well. Someone in the crowd asked if Mợ Hà was my mother and I replied "no, she was my stepmother". Now the crowd that had gathered turned against Mợ Hà and one of the women in the crowd held me to her. She told Mợ Hà to return home with the money she had made from selling my sister and tell my father what had happened. The woman said that when he returned she would hand me over to him, not her. I heard the woman say that she was afraid that left with Mợ Hà I would be sold to a merchant, who would sell me on as a slave in China. Mợ Hà was given food and clothes and time to calm herself, and also told where I would be staying so she had confidence in leaving me.

A kind stranger

The kind woman who had helped me sold cơm bụi (dusty food, i.e. the cheapest food, sold by hawkers on the street) at the station. But when Mợ Hà had gone I was taken to another lady who lived near the market to help her look after her children and husband, who was blind. The two children were very young and the lady was herself blind in one eye. Her house was extremely dirty and the husband frightened me. I'd never seen a blind person before. The woman sold cháo lòng (rice porridge with intestines). Her name was Co Liên (Aunt Lien) and I was told to stay with her and await my father's return. But I refused to stay and asked the kind woman if I could stay with her instead. She replied that she already had four children and didn't need any more. But I pleaded with her and said that I would only stay with her, and not with this new family. At this she laughed, and said that she'd already told me that this was impossible.

But eventually my pleading seemed to work, and she told me that I'd better follow her out of Co Liên's house. We walked straight to the public tap, where she gave me a wash, along with some clothes to wear. She even brushed my hair and I can remember her saying there were so many nits they were like figs in a tree – too many to count.

For the rest of the day I stayed with her while she sold food. I felt safe. The kind woman took me home when she finished work that night. Home was a single-room house and when we arrived the rest of the family were already in bed and I was told to find a place on the floor to sleep. The woman said she would tell the other family members about me in the morning.

When I awoke she introduced me to the rest of the family and told me that I would be staying with them. I told them my name and from that moment on I was – at least temporarily – part of their family.

The children's grandmother also lived at the house, and I was told that my job was to help her with the housework. The old lady did all of this, as I quickly learned none of the four children did anything to help. They were all younger than me, and all went to school. Despite our age difference, I was the smallest.

I quickly settled into a routine and was happy in this secure environment, away from the far greater hardships and dangers of my previous life. My new life was hard, and of course I never forgot that I wasn't a proper member of the family, but I felt as though I was at least safe among them.

As time went on the old lady's health began to deteriorate and I started to do more and more of the housework. I had become the family's ô xin[5] (housemaid), and this is how I was introduced to anybody we met. One of the many jobs I was tasked with was

---

[5] It was at the time, and still is, very common in Việt Nam for families of even modest means to employ somebody to work as the family maid. Maids would normally start as young children, and would often be a poor relative from the countryside. They would receive food and have a place to sleep (often a space on a bed or mat on the floor, shared with the family's children). Ô xin often wouldn't receive a wage – it was considered enough that they were given food to eat and shelter.

washing the family's clothes, which involved going to the public tap — often with a pile of clothes taller than me. It was extremely hard, physical work.

Once washed, I'd have to climb the rickety old bamboo ladder with the bucket of heavy wet clothes to hang them out on the roof. I had to be so careful where I trod for fear of falling through that roof, and was always relieved when I'd finished. But despite the dangers with this or other tasks I never complained. I knew that I had no option but to accept any job I was given.

My world at this time was very small, involving little more than the alleyway that the family's house was in. Even though I was given more freedoms here, I was careful not to roam further than I considered safe. But one day I was given the family's food 'token', which allowed recipients to buy a few kilogrammes of discounted rice from the government store. This involved a walk to the main road at the end of the alleyway, and was somewhere I had yet to venture.

As I approached the road, Phố Hàng Bột, the noise was the first thing to strike me. I looked left and right and saw shops on either side of the road as far as I could see. The road itself was full of bicycles, cyclos and the occasional motorcycle, but I instinctively stepped on to it knowing that were I to walk on the pavement dressed in the rags I was wearing I would be shooed away by shopkeepers, who would think I was either a thief or a beggar. So I shuffled along the road next to the curb, fascinated by all of the goods for sale. There were shops selling electrical items, clothes and food – and I especially remember one that sold sweet-smelling phở[6] from a huge, steaming pot.

I continued along the road, making my way towards the government store that sold rice, but became transfixed by a shop selling televisions. I had glanced at one before, with its tiny screen, but here the TVs were bigger, and there were lots of them. I gazed at the flickering black-and-white images, imagining that the scenes were real. I was unaware of the bell being frantically rung on the approaching tram.

The next thing I remember was a rough hand grabbing me and pulling me on to the pavement. As I stood staring at the tram that had sped past, narrowly missing me, the stranger who had saved me blurted out "cháu có muốn chết, không?" (do you want to die, child?). I had no idea what a tram was. I certainly had no idea that I had been walking along its tracks.

Visitors

I carried on this way for at least a couple of years when one day, after I had washed all of the family's clothes and was preparing for lunch, my 'adoptive' mother arrived home with Mợ Hà and my father. She said that they had come to take me home. For a moment I froze, before turning to my adoptive mother and insisting that I wanted to stay with her in Hà Nội – even though they had never offered to keep me permanently. My life as an ô xin was tough, but I knew it was so much better than the life I

---

[6] Phở, or noodle broth, is almost the national dish of Việt Nam, eaten at all times of the day.

could ever have in the village. The fact was I hadn't been beaten for two years now, and I never wanted to be beaten again.

Recognising my reluctance to leave, my father said that if I wanted to stay in Hà Nội I should at least return to the village for a visit. He spoke calmly and reassuringly, and I eventually agreed to what seemed to be a small concession. I had never heard him speak so gently. So, after we had eaten some lunch together with my adoptive family I went with my father and Mợ Hà to start our journey back to my home village. Although I was full of trepidation – even fear – as to what might happen, I was also slightly excited at the prospect of going home and seeing my brother and sisters, even if it was only briefly.

When we arrived home my excitement was short-lived, for it quickly became clear that nothing in the village had changed for the better and, if anything, had only gotten worse. For the first day or two my father continued to treat me well. But quickly the veneer began to peel, and what emerged was worse than I had ever experienced. Now father seemed to have even more fury – and he constantly berated and abused Mợ Hà, blaming her for destroying his family; blaming her for losing me and Luyến; and accusing her of having another man's child. After all, how was it possible to have given birth to so many daughters when all he had wanted was another son? She turned black and blue before my eyes and stayed that way for the next few months.

This was clearly not going to be the short visit home I had been promised. I was trapped again and, far from returning to Hà Nội to resume my work as an ô xin, I now had to stay and watch the constant abuse of my stepmother. Of course father had had no intention of allowing me to return to Hà Nội – I had realised that very quickly. In the event I had to endure another two years of village life under his rule.

This was a scary and upsetting time for me. As well as missing my life in Hà Nội I was also missing my elder sister, Liên. It was only upon my return to the village that I had found out that she had also run away from home. I hadn't been told this in Hà Nội. To this day I don't know for sure what made her leave, but I can imagine how terrible things must have been for my siblings while I'd been away in Hà Nội. I've always been aware that as grim as my treatment has been at the hands of my father I have always been his favourite child. My elder siblings had it worse than me.

It was undoubtedly his need of another pair of working hands that eventually drove father to try and find me. Although in such a chauvinistic society as (especially) rural Việt Nam was at this time, where daughters were considered of little value[7], he nevertheless knew my worth as a worker – and he needed to have workers around him to provide for his needs. I imagine he would have eventually forced Mợ Hà to tell him where she had abandoned me in Hà Nội, and had decided that it was worth the effort to at least try and find me.

And so we continued in this way. Hard work, hunger and beatings, until eventually Mợ Hà could stand it no longer and she fled to her home village with Ly and Liễu, her biological children. I later found out that upon her return she had been

---

[7] Males in general were valued as being far superior to women at this time – hence the expression 'a hundred women aren't equal to the single testicle hair of a man', which father would often repeat.

rejected by her family as she was considered to have already left the family home to be with her husband. It mustn't have helped her case that she had arrived with two dependents in tow. Mợ Hà's only option was to work as a labourer for a neighbour.

That left me and my brother, Long. It meant that there were now only two of us left in the house to feel the brunt of father's anger. Long had by far the worst of it and was regularly severely beaten.

Long was a good brother and he did his best to look out for me. Apart from father, my biggest terror as a youngster was having to go outside into the night to do a wee in the garden. It was a haven for all kinds of animals, including my worst fear of all – snakes. When I needed to go I would beg Long or Mợ Hà to take me outside, which they normally would. But if they weren't around I would simply wet myself rather than run the risk of being bitten.

Long was hard-working and managed all of our land. We had about a hectare of rice paddy, although this was not enough to sustain a family. In the times when we were not working on the land we were sent out to find food. From wet land this would include small fish, eels, snails or frogs – anything that we could eat, or sell if there was a surplus[8]. We were given bits of food by my father, once he had eaten his fill. We were made to work constantly.

---

[8] Because of our poor diet we were prone to having intestinal worms. I can remember one crawling out of my mouth, and one from by backside, on two occasions. Each year we would have a worming tablet to rid them from our systems.

One day, father started to dig a well in our garden. We had already made the bricks for the sides. It was hard, physical work and we were too hungry to carry it out properly. It took weeks of work to reach the ground water, with the rough brick and mortar cylinder sections lowered down on ropes. In the end it must have been nearly ten metres deep. As the well got deeper so did my yearning to run away. I couldn't tell Long, as I knew he would have stopped me – and probably beaten me for suggesting such a terrible thing – but once the well was finished I took advantage of a rare opportunity when my father was in a good mood. I asked if I could walk to my cousin's house nearby as they had a TV. He didn't answer, which was his way of saying 'yes'. But instead of going to my cousin's house I called on my neighbour and asked if I could hide from my father there. I asked my neighbour to take me to anybody who knew the whereabouts of my sister, Liên. My neighbour told me to return home as he was afraid my father would find out where I was and there would be big trouble between them. I asked that I be allowed to stay hidden in their kitchen covered in hay and he could take me in the morning. I begged him to help and refused to leave his house. Eventually, he told me to hide in the kitchen as I had suggested, and said that he would see in the morning what he could do.

At around three to four o'clock in the morning he told me to jump on to his bicycle and he cycled for an hour or so until we reached the house of a lady who, it turned out, was the wife of my father's cousin. My neighbour explained the situation and said that I was desperate to meet my sister. He returned home. The lady asked if I knew where Liên was, and where I had been when Liên had run away. She made me promise that if she helped I wouldn't tell anybody that she had stepped in. When I agreed, she told me to run down the lane and said she would keep up with me, with a safe enough distance between us. To walk with me was clearly too dangerous as the news may have got back to my father. Everybody feared my father.

So I ran and ran. When I couldn't see the lady any more I would hide in a patch of roadside scrub and wait for her to appear. Eventually, I came to a river crossing and a small ferry was waiting to set off. It was full of people heading to market, many carrying vegetables or fruit on bamboo poles or strapped to bicycles. I jumped on to the ferry without asking and, fortunately, nobody mentioned a ticket. They would have assumed I had no money in any case. I looked up and was relieved to see the lady was also on board. When the ferry reached the other bank I jumped off and continued down the road, eventually coming to a small development with what looked to be a coach station.

Guessing this was our destination I waited for the lady to catch up. There was a single coach parked at the station and once she had reached me she told me to slip on to it, without being seen, and hide under a seat. She was clearly still afraid that my father would be out searching for me. The coach began to fill with passengers and then we were under way. As the coach pulled off the woman came to find me, and then we sat together. I looked out of the coach window in the direction of my father's house, searching for the huge eucalyptus tree in our garden. But all I could think of was the terrible fate awaiting my brother, who was now on his own with my father. I was terrified that he was already being beaten by him if he thought that Long had helped me to escape. But I had to hide even these tears, because I couldn't risk the woman thinking that I missing home.

The next thing I knew was that the coach was stopping on the outskirts of a big city, next to a rusty old bridge[9]. After buying me something to eat we walked along a busy road to a market near to the river. It was quite a walk but at least I had eaten something. When we reached the market I was amazed to see so many animals for sale, some of them looked to be rare creatures – monkeys, snakes and other, strange-looking animals I'd never seen before. The lady said we needed to buy some groceries and I told her that I thought I had been here before. I guessed we were in Hà Nội, and said that I thought we were near to the home of my adoptive parents. She asked me if I wanted to visit them or carry on to visit Liên. After telling her that I still wanted to be with Liên we returned to the bus stop at the bridge and caught another coach. I had no idea where to but after a few hours travelling we were passing through mountain valleys as the evening approached.

Eventually the coach came to a stop and we stepped off. Once again I was surrounded by hills and mountains. There were trees everywhere and very few huts, and the land seemed to be of poor quality – none of the lush green fields I was used to seeing. I was scared now as I realised I was with a stranger and she could be taking me anywhere. For about an hour we walked along stony paths and crossed many fields. We eventually arrived at a fine-looking house, which is to say it was built from concrete and, unlike our hut, had a tiled roof. Trees surrounded the house and there were chickens and pigs in the yard. It looked prosperous. My heart leaped when my sister emerged

---

[9] The bridge was the famous Long Biên Bridge, which at the time was the main link between the city and Gia Lam district across the Red River.

from the house. Liên, who was an ô xin for the family and their two children (one her age, one younger), looked stunned when she saw me and the two of us stood like statues staring at each other, overwhelmed by the reunion. We didn't hug or even hold hands as we weren't used to showing emotion.

The lady who had brought me to meet Liên left the following morning. For two or three days I stayed with my sister and the family who had taken her in. I told her of my life with my adoptive family in Hà Nội and how good it had been. I told her how happy I had been there. But I also said that if she returned to our village our father would surely change his ways. I desperately wanted Liên to return to the village with me. I'd somehow convinced myself that father could change if only all of the siblings were reunited under one roof. Liên was very sceptical at first, but listened attentively and, after much thought, was eventually persuaded by my argument. And so, after a further few days working for the family, we started out on our return journey to the village, using the little money that Liên had been given by the family she had been working for whenever we couldn't beg for rides. I guess I was 13 at this point. Liên was a year older.

We walked for miles, rode for some more on the back of kind strangers' bicycles, and caught coaches when we had to. When we eventually arrived at our village we walked slowly along the dusty track to father's house, and stopped to open the creaky bamboo gate. Nervously, we walked into the courtyard. The scene that greeted us was typical: father was sat at the table drinking stewed green tea. He was silent, and just stared at us. For an hour or so he said nothing, before eventually turning to us and demanding to know where we had been and why we had returned home.

It was clear that the return of Liên had had the opposite effect to the one I had hoped for. We explained the whole story – that all I had wanted to do was to find Liên, bring her home and unite the family. But he screamed that he didn't want children who didn't respect him. He said that we had treated him as if he wasn't our father, and therefore he would act in the same way.

Eventually the commotion began to draw the neighbours, and one by one they began to gather, intrigued by what had caused Lập[10] to shout. More and more people from the village arrived and our father became even more agitated. But the crowd was too big for him to be seen hitting us and he eventually grabbed our arms and pulled us on to the road outside, before returning through the gate to the house. We took our chances and tried to blend in with the crowd to hide from him.

After some time father re-emerged with a small bowl full of grains of salt and rice. This is what you would offer the dead and you cast the grains and salt over the bodies to give them something to eat on their journey into the afterlife. He threw it over us. It was the ultimate rejection and Liên and I received it publically. Liên decided there and then to leave once more. I was desperate to stay with her but she refused. She shouted at me, saying it was a big mistake listening to me in the first place and told me to stay. But I refused. I ran along with her until she stopped, turned towards me and furiously slapped me. She was angry and desperate to escape the village and the humiliation,

---

[10] Lập is my father's name. In the village he is now known as Ông Lập (Old Man Lap) and is known as the curmudgeonly old man.

and she clearly thought that I would only hinder her. But I refused to listen and clung to her like a limpet.

Liên asked some villagers if they knew where our biological mother's village was. We had never visited it and didn't even know its name. The people, who knew our family, told us where it was, what it was called and how we could get there. Liên must have decided that her only real hope of escape was to make it to our mother's relatives, and so she started walking in the direction the villagers had suggested, with me still clinging to her. We walked and walked on the track out of our village until we came to a main road, where we saw a man standing waiting for a xe lam (motorised three-wheeled vehicle, a bit like a tuk-tuk). We asked for his help with directions, to check that the first set of directions had been correct. Neither Liên nor I could read so we knew we were dependent on the help of others if we were to successfully navigate our way to our mother's village.

We would follow directions for as long as we could remember them, always checking with others we came across along the way that we were heading in the right direction. The popular method of travel in rural areas like ours at that time was the xe lam. If one came along that wasn't too full we would try and hitch a ride. It was such a relief when one pulled over, and we were lucky to have a few rides that day. We still weren't talking, but at least Liên seemed to have accepted me as a travelling companion.

On the last xe lam we hitched a lift on we noticed that there was a bulging plastic bag next to us that nobody seemed to own. When it was time to jump off the driver asked if it was ours and we said no. None of the other passengers claimed it as theirs' so the driver told us to take it. When we jumped off the xe lam and peeked inside we couldn't believe our luck. There were fried spring rolls, along with sticky rice wrapped in banana leaf, and boiled chicken. Such a selection of delicacies must have belonged to a guest at a celebration, possibly a wedding. The food was even still slightly warm.

In those days it would only have been a very special occasion such as this that such food was prepared. We looked at each other, smiled, and found a place to sit and eat. It was the most delicious food we had ever eaten – heavenly – and it had been left in the back of a xe lam. After our meal Liên's mood greatly improved and she began to open up and talk to me. It was the first time we had spoken since leaving our home.

We carried on looking for our grandmother's village – all we knew was that she lived with our uncle. We knew that it involved crossing a river and had to beg our passage across it when eventually we came upon a ferry. The river was wide and powerful – swollen after heavy rain. It took about 30 minutes or so until we reached the stop that the passengers on the ferry said we needed. The passengers said that once we had disembarked we simply had to follow the road we would be on, which would take us straight to our grandmother's village. It was a journey of only three or four miles, but it seemed much further to us. Our legs were short and we were tired after the events of the long day. To make matters worse it was a very quiet road and there was hardly any traffic, so our opportunities for a lift were few. Eventually a lady who was cycling past stopped to ask who we were, and we asked if she knew the village we were looking for. Her black, loose-fitting trousers and blouse that had long ago been white were typical for the time, as was the nón (conical hat) she wore, and scarf that covered her neck and mouth, leaving only her nose and eyes exposed. It must have been late afternoon, for had it have been sunny the scarf would surely have covered her nose as well[11]. The lady said that she was going there herself and asked who we were looking for. When we told her she asked if our mother was called Mẹ Bảy (Mother Number Seven). It was our mother's name. To our surprise she clearly knew our family – and even said that I looked like my mother.

It transpired that the lady had gone to school with our mother when she was very young – and she told us to jump on her bike, one at a time. She would cycle for a while and drop off whoever was on the bicycle, before returning for whoever had been left behind. She kindly shuttled us this way all the way to our grandmother's house, and then stood at the gate calling out to see if anybody was home, as was customary. "Your grandchildren are visiting – Mẹ Bảy's daughters".

Our grandmother's house looked good to us – much better than our father's. It turned out it had been newly built by our uncle and looked luxurious by our standards. It was made of concrete, and it was large. Our uncle came down the path to the gate and asked if we were Liên and Lan. He seemed happy to see us and invited us in to the house, where our grandmother was sitting on a wooden bench. It was the first time we'd ever seen her, and she seemed warm and friendly, smiling at us and flashing a set of teeth already stained black through years of chewing betel nut. It

---

[11] As is still the case, women didn't like to expose themselves to sunlight as the resulting darker skin made them look like they worked the fields and were therefore nhà quê (had a home in the countryside – i.e. country bumpkins).

was a warm reception and as good as we could have possibly hoped for.

Liên and I sat down and we told my uncle and grandmother what had happened and what had brought us to their home. They listened carefully to our story. We were made to feel welcome and they agreed that we could stay for a short time.

Life was good here and we quickly settled into a routine. The village life was familiar to us but now, instead of working all hours for little food and regular beatings, we were rewarded for helping the family with the farm work by good food and warmth. Meals were generally twice a day and involved rice with vegetables and broth[12], but we would sometimes have eggs or tofu. Very occasionally we would even have meat. We were happy and had it have been up to us would surely have stayed here in this secure bubble. But after around one month our uncle said that Liên had to leave — to stay with somebody he knew very well who needed a helper. She lived in a mountainous area and had a son. As I was the youngest I was allowed to stay with my grandmother, for the time being at least.

Liên left and a few months passed until one day a visitor to my grandmother's house arrived. Apparently, she was a distant cousin. Standing in the brick courtyard to the front of the house she looked up and saw me standing in the doorway, and asked excitedly if I was Bẩy's daughter. Sitting on the bench while the customary green tea was being prepared the distant cousin asked my uncle and grandmother about my story, my situation, and

---

[12] Broth was, and essentially still is, the water that vegetables are boiled in. In the region my uncle's house was in this was typically morning glory, but would include any edible leaf from the garden.

afterwards enquired if I would like to go and live with her in Hải Phòng (the port city to the east of Hà Nội). Apparently, she needed help with her food stall. My uncle was clearly aware of this plan and said that I would have to go with her as life in the countryside was tough and he was finding it difficult providing for me as one of the family. Although I was sad I understood his position.

So that evening my uncle gave me some money: 7,000 đồng (about enough for 14 loaves of bread). Although I was sad to be leaving I was overjoyed as this was the most money I had ever had to my name. I set off with the visitor, who I addressed as Dì (Younger Aunt), on a coach to Hải Phòng. I gave Dì the money to hold as I had no pocket.

Hải Phòng

Dì lived with her husband in a simple, one-room flat in an area best described as a slum. But they had a room in which to sit and sleep in and a small makeshift kitchen area. Dì asked if I knew how to do anything and I told her of all the things I used to do for my adoptive family in Hà Nội. I think she was relieved.

Dì's business involved going to the market and buying pig skin and fat, with which she made a speciality dish of Hải Phòng: nem chao (crunchy pig skin with roasted rice powder – eaten with salad). Once home she would boil the pig skin and then put it into cold water to cool, before removing it and leaving it to dry. Once dry Dì put the skin into a big jar and placed it into a kind of liquid marinade, where it would stay overnight before being removed in the morning. Any fat left on the skin was then scraped away. My job was to take a pair of tweezers and remove any of the remaining hair. By 8am each morning Dì had to be ready to sell the skin, which she would hawk as a local dish. My next task was to prepare the herbs and salad leaves, which would be sold with the skin. As everything had to be as fresh as possible so that it would tempt customers, we were always in a rush.

While she was away selling the nem chạo in the city I would stay with her husband to clear up. About 300 metres from their flat was a communal tap, and I would go there to wash the clothes, a job I knew well from my time in Hà Nội, before returning to fill all of our water containers. As was typical of homes at the time there was no running water, or toilet. A wee would be done in the gutter, but anything else involved a trip to the nearby public toilet, which I dreaded because it was in an especially rough area and was filthy. You never knew who or what you would meet on the way. By 2pm I would be finished with all of the chores and would be home ready for Dì's return. She would return with the next day's skin for preparation and the whole process would repeat.

I stayed with Dì in Hải Phòng for about 10 months. I didn't have an issue with the work – if anything it was easier than it had been in Hà Nội. But I missed my life in the capital. In Hà Nội I had extra work, but I had freedom as well. In Hà Nội I had enough food to eat and I always seemed to be happy. I enjoyed helping people, and everybody seemed happy to see me whenever I was allowed out of the house.

In Hải Phòng, by contrast, the flat was very small, and I was the only child, with nobody to talk to. Although Dì's husband had a son – the result of an affair he had had – he was in prison while I lived with them, so it was just the three of us living together.

The public tap which we used was near the railroad track, and every time a train rumbled by I would find myself wondering where it was going. Eventually I asked somebody who was also waiting for the tap where the trains were headed. She told me it was Hà Nội. I asked others how I could get to the train station, and if I needed to change trains in order to get to Hà Nội. In the back of my mind I was beginning to wonder if I could possibly return to Hà Nội, and the life I missed.

One day Dì returned home earlier than usual and we ate earlier than we normally would, to allow her time to go to the temple to pray. By 8pm it was my bed time and I went into the corner of the room and pulled a blanket over my head, as was normal. But when Dì's husband came in to turn off the TV he came over to where I was and started to touch me. He worked his fingers up my leg, getting closer and closer, until he reached where he wanted to be. I turned to try to get away. All the time my heart was pounding, although I tried to at least appear asleep. I kept still and hoped in vain that Dì would return home. Finally, Dì returned and he left to go to bed.

The next day I didn't mention the incident to either Dì or her husband. I just continued on as usual. I was beyond embarrassed by what had happened to me and was fearful of what might happen to me if I said anything. In those days someone in my position was extremely vulnerable – and I knew that it was quite possible the husband would deny what had happened and I would be in big trouble. I knew though that I had to do something and soon after I came to the conclusion that I had to get away. I resolved to return to Hà Nội.

I asked again for directions to the station when I next went to the tap, and carried on saving the 500 đồng a day I was given by Dì for my breakfast. I had no idea how much a ticket was. But I did know where Dì kept her money (which she would have to hide from her husband as otherwise he, like many Vietnamese husbands, would have taken it to gamble with). I knew she had 7,000 đồng of mine, and I took this money when the husband wasn't looking. No more.

When Dì left the house on the day I had planned to escape I had to wait until about lunchtime before taking my opportunity to leave, quickly jumping into a cyclo and asking the rider to take me to the train station as fast as he could. I chose lunchtime because I knew Dì would be out of the house selling her food and her husband would be taking his mid-day nap. Also, it would not be unusual at this time for me to be outside the house – usually to fill the water containers. When I left the house I had no bag, just the clothes I was wearing. I could hardly wait to jump out of the cyclo when we pulled up outside Hải Phòng train station, and I ran straight to the ticket office clutching the money I had remaining. I was terrified as I approached the counter and asked for a ticket to Hà Nội, and was crest-fallen when the ticket seller said that I was a few hundred đồng short of the total I needed.

But my mood went from despair to elation when the woman standing behind me in the queue lent over and kindly agreed to pay the extra money. She had young children in tow and I asked if she was heading to Hà Nội, which she said she was. As I knew the woman was going to my intended destination I decided to keep her in sight, and even sat opposite her on the train. As we pulled out of Hải Phòng she must have noticed that I had no food, and she kindly gave me a biscuit – still in a wrapper. I thanked her and kept the biscuit. As tempted as I was to eat such a delicacy I didn't once think of doing so, preferring instead to keep it as a potential present – an offering to give to somebody once I had arrived in Hà Nội.

Back to Hà Nội

When we reached Hà Nội I ran as quickly as possible from the station, hoping to see my adoptive mother at her stall. But it was the afternoon – at the time when people tended to sleep – and I could only spot one lady I recognised, who was sat inside the station compound selling cơm bình dân (simple food). I remembered my biscuit and quickly offered it as a gift – and asked the woman if she knew where my adoptive mother was. She did, and what's more she took me straight to her. My gift had worked.

As soon as I saw my adoptive mother I couldn't contain myself and sprinted towards her to give her a tight hug. As I threw my arms around her I asked why she had ever let me go. It was early 1992, or thereabouts, so I would have been 14 by this time.

Again I was taken in by the family and I returned to my job as their ô xin. It was timely for the family as by now the grandmother's curvature of the spine was worse and within a few months she sadly died. She had never had a cross word with me and I liked the old lady and her kindness. I remember that she would constantly re-read a religious text whenever the work was done. What she found in it I don't know but I guess it must have given her some reassurance. With the old lady gone, all of the housework now passed to me.

At home the children were bigger and older now and they began to bully me more as they were fully aware I was only the maid. I had to learn to protect myself as best I could. Up to this point the siblings had abused their power relationship with me – making me do things I didn't want to do. There were small indignities like farting in my face, but it was the more subtle abuses that were the most undermining. Chief among them was the fact that, although younger than me, I had to refer to them as anh, chị (older brother and sister). In Việt Nam respect is given to those older than you and this system is rigid. You must refer to somebody by the correct title. This meant that every single time I referred to the siblings I confirmed to them and to myself that I had an inferior status[13]. My only solace was to point out to them, whenever the opportunity presented itself, that I could do things they couldn't. I may have been a nhà quê (the insulting term meaning country bumpkin that they called me), but I was far more competent at many things and I wanted them to know that they were dependent on me.

One day the siblings asked me to join their game of hide and seek, although even then they took the opportunity to belittle

---

[13] This situation continued until 2023, when I last went to visit them. I'd heard that their life had improved, and they were working at Lenin's Statue – renting out battery-powered cars for children to sit in and drive on the large expanse of paving in front of it. I would always look up the family when in Hà Nội. This time, without prompting, the tables were turned and they referred to me for the first time as chị. Finally, I was the older sister.

me by ignoring me when it was my turn to hide. So when it was my turn to find them I used the opportunity to hide from them instead. I wanted some time to myself. There was a corner of a room where all the clothes were hung and pans and crockery were kept. The other children were scared of this bit of the house, so I knew I would be undetected – for a while at least. As I hid I can remember suddenly feeling overwhelmed by the helplessness of my situation and I started to cry, uncontrollably. When eventually the others heard me sobbing, one of them called to a neighbour, as there was no adult in the house at the time.

I heard the siblings tell the neighbour that they had no idea why I was crying and she suggested that I may have been possessed by the ghost of my late mother. In Việt Nam the belief in spirits is very strong, so this would have had an impact on the siblings. The neighbour gave me something to eat and drink and spoke softly to reassure me. When, sometime later, my adoptive mother returned home and learned what had happened, she told me that I didn't have to do any more work that day.

It seemed that, however briefly and for whatever reason, my status within the family had somehow changed. I quickly realised that there could be an opportunity to make this arrangement more permanent – and there was only way I could think of to achieve this. I looked up at my adoptive mother and called to her "mẹ" (mother). I had never done this before and had no way of knowing how she would respond. Had she have scolded me then my opportunity would have gone, but she did not object – and later that day I called my adoptive father "bố" (father). Why they accepted this I don't know. Perhaps they were afraid of a ghost.

What I do know is that from this point on, although my workload remained the same, I felt a bit more secure within the family. By referring to them as mum and dad I had more standing and knew the siblings could no longer bully me in the same way as before.

Back in Hà Nội the biggest change in my immediate surroundings was the queue for the public tap. It was bigger than ever and there seemed to be more clothes than ever to wash and more water to collect.

I can remember on one occasion the father decided that the children needed a wash as they had been out playing in the rain. In those days the streets were particularly filthy and the children were covered in dirt.

As usual I filled the tub with water, but in no time at all the water containers were empty and I was sent out with buckets for more. Fortunately, as it was raining the queue for the tap was smaller. Each time I returned home with the buckets of water I would have to plunge a heating element into one of the buckets. This would very often spark when I plugged it in – a task made all the more dangerous by the fact that my hands were soaking wet[14]. It was such a scary thing to do, and I would always try and push the plug into the socket as quickly and lightly as possible – a difficult task as the socket was too loose to properly grip the plug. I was particularly scared because I knew that my mother had died of an electric shock when I was a young child. On this occasion I struggled to get the element to heat and my adoptive

---

[14] Heating elements where similar to those found in a kettle, and would be placed directly into a container of water – making sure that the electric cable didn't touch the water. There was no earth.

father got increasingly angry because he said I wasn't doing it properly. The children's water was getting cold. But when he forced me to hold the plug tightly as I attempted to plug it in I had an electric shock from the sparking socket. In those days there were no safety devices on electrical circuits so the shock continued until I dropped the element. I burst into tears and said that I couldn't do as he had told me to do. But this only served to make the father angry, and I watched in horror as he took out a fruit knife and threw it straight at me. Although the blade was only a few inches long fruit knives are extremely sharp and it pierced my leg with ease. I looked down and saw it sticking out from my calf muscle. I still have the scar.

I looked at the father and he was clearly upset by what he had done. I think he must have instantly regretted his actions as he said he was going to bathe me once the children had finished in the tub. He had never done that before. Although I felt very uncomfortable with this thorough wash, from that point on he was always much more gentle with me, and was never again violent.

A couple of perks

Although much of this work was hard and tedious, there was at least one job that I always enjoyed. This involved washing the grass mats that the family used to sleep on. I could remember the women in my home village doing this – and remembered the snapping noise as the wet mats were slapped across hard ground to rid them of excess water. I was eager to try this for myself. Once soaking wet I would roll the mats into tubes and brush them with soapy water to remove the ingrained dirt. It was hard work but fun, because at the end I would be as soaking as the mats had been and I was allowed to wash myself.

Another job with a benefit was acting as look-out when the father was gambling with his friends. Like many families, the father – even though he didn't earn money – loved to gamble with his wife's when she had any. Of course in Việt Nam at the time this was strictly illegal and I was an important part of proceedings, propped against the front door frame with a blanket covering me, keeping an eye trained down the alleyway for any wandering police. The gambling would often go on until midnight, well after the children were in bed, and I would be rewarded for my efforts by the gamblers with a little money that I would use to buy a simple breakfast.

The night shift

Time went on and at the end of the following year I was told that it was time for me to have a new role in the household. At the time my adoptive mother used to sell food she had prepared from a stall in the station compound. She would work through the day, returning home at around 8pm, often with food remaining that would be sold the next day if it was still deemed edible. It was never good food, even when freshly cooked. My adoptive mother told me that from now on I would have far fewer housekeeping duties, and instead I would take over the stall from her once she had finished her day shift and sell the food through the night. It was a way that the family could earn much-needed extra money. I usually worked from around 8pm until about 6.30am – unless the food had sold out earlier – returning home with the table of remaining food after asking a fellow trader for help carrying it.

The station compound was a chaotic mix of hawkers selling their goods, travellers killing time before their trains arrived, and the usual collection of black marketeers and pickpockets. The black marketeers would attempt to pursued unsuspecting travellers to pay a premium for the tickets they held – hoping to convince them that they were the only tickets left available for their trains.

My job was to sit at the table and call out to passers-by as the food warmed, praying all the while that it didn't rain as I had no cover. I sold a mixture of cold dishes (cơm bình dân)[15]. Although I was really pleased with this at first as I thought it was nice to be trusted – and I had far less housework to do – I did wonder why the family's eldest child hadn't been given the job. When it rained there was a mad scramble to shelter in the station building – and I would have to beg for help from somebody to help carry my table.

It didn't take long to realise that it was extremely boring and frustrating working through the night. The novelty of being trusted quickly wore off. I had to stay put at the stall and stay awake – and the food was almost never fresh enough to be considered reasonable, which made it especially difficult to sell. My adoptive mother would sell the food at its freshest during the daytime, and even then it was poor quality. I was selling the leftovers that she had been unable to sell. Despite this I was always disappointed with myself if I returned home with unsold food, and my adoptive mother would sometimes accuse me of

---

[15] Other dishes included slow-cooked, salty fish, fried cheap cuts of meat, morning glory, fermented cabbage stir fried in lard, bamboo shoots and fried tofu in tomato sauce. The ingredients were always the cheapest available at the market.

sleeping instead of selling it – insisting that the whole family depended on me. Sometimes she would ask why the neighbouring stall had managed to sell all of their food and I hadn't. I felt terrible whenever I was accused of this. The truth was, though, that my neighbour's food was better than ours. Also, they looked smarter and gave customers more confidence, whereas our food was really unappealing – there only to make a quick profit with minimal outlay. I – the person selling the food – was always tatty, often not very clean and looked anything but professional. Basically, my adoptive mother hoped to rip people off who had travelled into the city from the countryside and weren't familiar with 'city ways'.

My best chance of attracting custom was if the neighbouring stall was busy with well-dressed people. When this happened customers who were dressed more like me would come to my stall – presumably thinking that the busy stall with well-dressed clientele was too expensive, or they were too embarrassed to sit next to smartly dressed people.

Despite the limitations and poor-quality food I had to work with, selling in this way gave me a valuable window on to the world and offered me opportunities that I would not have had were I to have stayed in the house doing only housework. It was valuable to me to be able to observe how 'normal' people reacted and responded to things. Even at an early age I knew that I suffered from big gaps in my upbringing that limited my experience of how to act among people, and I already knew that to be ignorant was a dangerous thing. Knowledge was power, especially when you were at the bottom of the ladder. When you lived the life I did you had to adapt quickly to survive, using the power of observation and experience. Of course, this was never taught to me.

At the station, I started to use such observations to my advantage by developing my own techniques for selling the food. Sat at the stall watching people decide where or what they were going to eat I realised quickly that some customers couldn't afford to pay for full portions – even of my food – and so I started to offer smaller amounts for a bit less money. This worked – and at least at first I started to bring in a bit more money for the family.

My adoptive family always lived hand-to-mouth and, if sales of the food had been poor, would have to either borrow money, or buy food at the market by promising to pay later. This was a very common practice at the time, and many people were almost permanently in some form of debt – my adoptive parents included.

After finishing my night shift I would return home at around 6.30-7am to start helping with the family's chores. Even though I had fewer jobs to do in the house, there was still a morning of work and I would only get to sleep at around noon.

If there was a best thing about this job it was that occasionally I could eat some of the food. Even if it wasn't the best, and it was truly far from it, it was still at least food and sometimes there was quite a lot of it. I don't think my adoptive mother ever noticed that I'd eaten something as she never commented on any missing food. I was always happiest eating anything when I'd had a good night of selling though – feeling as though I deserved a treat.

Ten dollars

I sold food for the next year, and by now I was around 15 years of age, although in truth I looked much younger. On one very quiet night I covered my food and wandered over to talk with a lady who sold phở outside the station to regular Hanoians, rather than the country travellers who I sold to. Her name was Tuyết (Snow). From that point on I would often talk with her whenever I had no customers. One night I was sat at her stall when a Western man stopped for a bowl of phở. He asked Tuyết why I was still up and was not in bed as by then it was the early hours of the morning. She tried to tell him that, like her, I also sold food during the night. When he had paid for the phở he turned to me and gave me a US$10 note. The stallholder said he had told me to go home to sleep. I was so happy. I bowed my head and said "cảm ơn" (thank you). When the man had gone, Tuyết said that I could go to the gold shop in the morning and change the note into Vietnamese currency. She said it was worth 90,000 đồng.

On that day I hadn't sold anything at all but I was delighted to return home with the tale of the $10 note. I told my adoptive mother that I wanted to use the money to buy material to make some trousers for myself, which was my dream. I couldn't wait to head to the gold shop to exchange the note for đồng, and on the way home I treated myself to a lovely bowl of beef phở. It cost 1,500 đồng. What a treat. The material for the trousers cost 45,000 đồng, and I was told it would cost an extra 15,000 đồng for labour. That still left nearly 30,000 đồng.

My adoptive mother said that I could keep the money for the material but I had to give her the remainder so that she could buy food in the meantime. Remember, things were so tight that she often had to borrow money for the next day's food, so I wasn't surprised by this, and furthermore she reassured me that she would give me the money for the seamstress when I needed it. I was still happy to be able to give such a large amount of money to her and had no regrets about handing it over. I went to the market and gave the material to the dress-maker, who said the trousers would be ready in three days' time.

I was so excited after the three days were up and couldn't wait to ask my adoptive mother for the 15,000 đồng outstanding. But she said she hadn't sold enough food the previous day and didn't have any money to give me at that time. So that evening I tried my best to sell as much food as possible so that she would have money to give me, but again the next day she said that she still didn't have enough. This went on day after day until I eventually realised that she had no intention of returning the 15,000 đồng I needed. I never did get the money and – of course – I never got to wear my lovely trousers.

In the meantime stories had begun to circulate in our neighbourhood about the $10, but the rumours were that I must have turned to prostitution to get so much money from a foreigner. It was such a bitter lesson for me and I felt really let down by it. Around the station there were many thieves and prostitutes, so it was awful to be labelled with the same tag after this man's simple act of generosity. And worse was to follow, because the rumour mongers said that Tuyết, who sold phở, must also be a prostitute because she too worked through the night. I felt so bad that I never returned to Tuyết's stall for fear

47

that I would make life difficult for her, and encourage the spread of more malicious rumours. That something so innocent – the kindness of a stranger – had caused such upset was hard to reconcile.

Life in the alleyways of Hà Nội was slowly beginning to teach me that if you were quiet and didn't react in the face of abuse, you would only receive more. It was a lesson I was to learn time and again.

Bear head

Life at the station changed dramatically between day and night, especially for the criminals and the kind of criminal activity that took place. Daytime was the time for pickpockets, who would wait for the next train to arrive and note carefully where each departing traveller likely kept anything of value – typically in shirt pockets. Often the pickpockets would pose as cyclo riders and, under the pretence of touting for custom, would manhandle people departing the station and discretely take whatever they had had their eyes on. The pickpockets would work in gangs, and there were several in the area. Sometimes the police would walk by to make the gangs know they were around. But the presence of the police wouldn't deter them as the pickpockets simply dispersed, only to quickly reform when the police left – like shoals of fish evading a passing shark.

I would often watch the gangs sharing their spoils. Whoever had made the grab would get the lion's share of the takings. Everybody who lived in the area knew who these gangs were and what they did but nobody said anything. Sometimes I would quietly warn my customers, the shabbily dressed country people, to be careful when they left my stall. I warned them not to talk to anybody.

At night the face of crime changed. There weren't as many trains so opportunities for pickpockets were fewer. The potential victims that were around were those passengers who were waiting for their morning trains, and most of them would rest in the station waiting room. Thieves would wander through the station and surrounding area looking for people who were sleeping with their belongings, hoping to snatch what they could without being spotted. Ironically, the thieves themselves were vulnerable as the area was controlled by a more dangerous đầu gấu gangster. He would oversee the handling of goods that passed through the station and was an official contractor. He was brutal. I once saw him forcing a youngster to hold his hand flat on the ground before he brought a chair leg down on the thief's fingers. Another time he forced a thief to lift up his top and expose his bare midriff – before handing him a razor blade. The thief himself had to slice around his belly button – and was warned that he would lose an arm if he refused to comply. It was testament to his fearsome reputation that nobody ever refused. The đầu gấu lived in a splendid house in the neighbourhood. Everybody lived in fear of his disapproval.

The whole neighbourhood was rough. On one occasion a couple who sold food at the station started to argue. The argument got increasingly heated and they started throwing things at each other. The husband raised a small knife and took aim at the woman. My adoptive mother shouted that he better not throw the knife near me as he was aiming near to us. But he didn't listen and the knife struck my head. Although I was injured by the knife and bleeding it wasn't what I would call serious. It did though leave a scar on the side of my head that I still bear. Later that day the couple came to my adoptive mother's stall with a bag of oranges and sugar as recompense for me.

The alley

In my free time I would play with my friends in the alleyway next to my adoptive family's house. We all lived in the alleyway – a dark and dingy space where the houses were little more than slum dwellings. Unlike the houses in my home village they were however made of concrete – some painted with simple lime-wash. Underfoot, the alleyway itself was compacted dirt which would quickly turn to mud when it rained. If the rain was heavy there'd be a small flood. But despite this the alley was my kingdom. Sometimes I'd meet my friends on their way to the tap to collect water or wash clothes; oftentimes I'd stay outside their front doors waiting for them to appear – hoping that their parents would allow me to sit on the step. I was rarely allowed inside, but sometimes I was allowed to sit and wait so long as I was quiet and didn't disturb their children. The parents knew that although I didn't go to school like their children I was at least hard-working. As such I was used as something of a warning for their offspring, who were told that unless they worked hard at school they would have a life like mine.

Although I couldn't follow my friends' conversations about their school lives, classmates and teachers, I was nevertheless proud of the fact that I had friends who went to school.

At that time my friends were everything I had. To be near them made me happy, and even though we didn't meet often I felt that our times shared were precious. Of course I know that they would have felt differently as their lives were relatively full of opportunity.

As hard as my life in Hà Nội was, relative to my life in the village it was full of positive things: I had clothes to wear and food to eat, I wasn't beaten, and − best of all − I didn't have to farm rice. This meant that I didn't have to fear being bitten by the leeches or snakes that lived in the paddy fields – the things I hated most of all. But although I felt as though my spirit was now that of a city-dweller, the people in the neighbourhood still called me by the derogatory term con bé nhà quê (child of the countryside).

The biggest difference between my life in the village and in Hà Nội was that now I knew that whatever work I did I would be rewarded in some little way for it – often some extra food to eat, possibly a piece of fruit or a sweet. Looking back I can see that the work I did kept me healthy – I was rarely sick.

At that time in Việt Nam even staple foods were often beyond people's means. Lucky households who were poor had tokens which allowed them to buy certain goods at discounted prices from government stores. My adoptive father's brother had been a soldier and lost his life, so their mother was given certain simple privileges. This might be some kilogrammes of rice or a couple of litres of kerosene. Kerosene was the fuel everybody used to cook with.

We would also cook with a single electric element, which sat in a kind of clay holding dish that pans could be placed on top of. Similar to my fears when heating the children's bath water, the prospect of an electric shock from the sparking socket terrified me. Of course the electricity in those days was straight from the mains, with none of the circuit breakers to protect users that you have nowadays. To make matters worse many people would use crocodile clips to attach a line to a section of stripped cable straight from the mains supply, which made it even more dangerous.

The family always seemed to be struggling for money. Like many families in Việt Nam, both then and now, the father did no work and everybody relied on the small amount earned by the mother at her food stall. If she had struggled to sell the food that day there would be little surplus to buy food to eat.

On such days a typical meal would be rice and peanuts. Because the nuts were more expensive than the rice every effort would be made to make them 'go further'. This involved cooking them in saltwater, with a small portion of fish sauce and monosodium glutamate poured in, which was bought from an old lady who sold such 'essentials' from a little stall in the alleyway.

Our family never bought a full bottle of sauce and had to rely on these small portions – often bought with an IOU for the next day. The water and fish sauce would be simmered away until the by-now sticky peanuts were left at the bottom of the pan. Super-salty they were the perfect accompaniment to the relatively bland, fluffy rice[16]. Although it was the most basic of foods, this dish was nevertheless always welcomed.

---

[16] Even today, making food extra salty in this way is a common way to make small portions, particularly of meat, seem more substantial. It works especially well with rice, which absorbs some of the saltiness.

A chance meeting

In Việt Nam, houses on any kind of road have greater value because they can be used to run businesses – especially shops. As the area around our house had slowly become more desirable, the value of my adoptive parent's house had increased. Eventually they decided to sell – and they bought a house in a much narrower alleyway, with less business potential. Luckily for me it wasn't too far away, although it was too far for me to maintain contact with my friends.

My life was largely unchanged, except for the fact that we now had a tap and a toilet in the house. The house itself was much bigger – and had two storeys and a mezzanine, although each floor was only one room. We still had no separate bedroom so, just as in the old house, when the family slept it was on grass mats on the floor. It was at least cleaner than the last house though because there was more space to store things.

The downside was that it was in a rougher area, although my family weren't scared of this fact. Nobody would ever mess with them as they were considered 'tough', and by now some of my adoptive siblings had left school and were hanging around with the roughest children in this new neighbourhood. Most were beginning a slow decline into a life of drugs and crime. One of the sons married at 16 and soon after was imprisoned. I was told he'd been caught stealing a bicycle, but even then I doubted this as his sentence was for 20 years. He was the second of the four children. The eldest daughter married a drug addict đầu gấu. The middle daughter was a drug addict who contracted and now lives with HIV. Her husband died of AIDS, a common fate for drug users at the time. The youngest daughter avoided drugs herself, although her husband was an addict.

There was one particularly nasty đầu gấu who was a regular visitor to the house. I knew from his reputation that he was dangerous and I knew – like all đầu gấu – his reputation for violence was everything to him. Without it he had nothing. One day he was teasing and threatening me in front of the siblings. Although I was scared of him I knew that I couldn't let it show. To do so would have handed him a victory as he would have known he intimidated me. Eventually he challenged me to a fight. I knew that I would have to come up with something quickly to avoid a potentially nasty beating. So, before he could move a muscle, I lunged at him and grabbed the bottom of his trouser legs to try and push him over, thinking that this would be the last thing he was expecting and it would give me time to run away. The problem was that, like many people at that time, his trousers weren't of the highest quality, so when I grabbed hold of them they began to tear. In a flash, and with a loud ripping sound, both trouser legs were shredded up to his crotch and the other children burst out laughing. I ran away of course and he chased me for a while, but the flapping material tangled in his legs and stopped him from running properly and catching me. As he ran the sound of laughter was ringing in my ears.

Despite the children's emerging problems, when we moved in to the new neighbourhood it seemed that the family's life was improving, if only by virtue of the fact the house was bigger. My life was very much the same – I still sold food at night, although now the family's frequent disappointment at my lack of success was getting me down. No matter what I did to try and improve sales, the fact remained the food I was attempting to sell was barely palatable – always made from the cheapest ingredients available.

One morning, as I was walking home from my night shift on the stall, I passed a lady who had been a neighbour at our previous address. She asked where I was going and how life was. I told her that things were difficult because I couldn't sell enough food and I was increasingly scared to return home. She said that if I, or anybody else I knew, wanted a job then there was an opportunity with her sister-in-law, who sold bia hơi (fresh beer – a Vietnamese institution). I asked for the name of the restaurant and the address. It seemed like a potential opportunity for me to make more money, which would help both me and my adoptive parents.

Later that morning, after telling the family that I hadn't made any money at all the night before, I hitched a lift to the area where the former-neighbour's sister-in-law sold beer. It was a quán ăn bình dân (simple restaurant) and when I arrived I told the woman that I had been given the address by her sister-in-law, who had told me there was an opening at the restaurant. The owner seemed friendly and I was really glad I had some sort of connection to her. She said I would be taken on for a monthly wage of 120,000 đồng (approximately £8) so long as I did okay in my first couple of days' work – my tasks including clearing tables, washing dishes and generally helping around the place.

When I returned home that afternoon I told my adoptive mother that I now had a job and didn't want to sell food for her any more. Despite the undoubted shock at this news she seemed okay with this idea, and so there and then the family stopped trying to sell food through the night using me to sell it. To be honest, by this time the money I was contributing by hawking food was so limited she was possibly relieved. The quality of the food she had been preparing had been steadily declining for a long time, and it had hardly been good to start with.

The first time I went to work at the restaurant I travelled pillion on the back of a bicycle, ridden by one of my adoptive brother's friends. I was full of trepidation and excitement at the prospect of earning some money for myself, and as we bumped along the main road on the old bicycle I knew that this was my opportunity to change my life for the better.

With my first wage packet I gave my adoptive mother 80,000 đồng and kept the 40,000 đồng to pay for breakfasts and travel to and from the restaurant on a xe lam. She was delighted with this.

In contrast to my frustrations trying to hawk the family's awful food, things now seemed to be going relatively well. I quickly settled into a new routine. Now, instead of my nocturnal existence where I was constantly at the beck and call of the family, I returned home only for sleeping, and was away from the house while the children slept. Starting work at 8am meant I had to leave at 7am. This suited me.

At the restaurant my first chores were preparing the food for the day ahead –typically fried noodles, dried or fresh, eel soup and

(Opposite). The first picture of me (right) with Long and Liên, taken in Lenin Park, Hà Nội. I would have been 17 at this time and had paid for the photo using my wages from the restaurant. It was taken by one of the many professional photographers who patrolled the park.

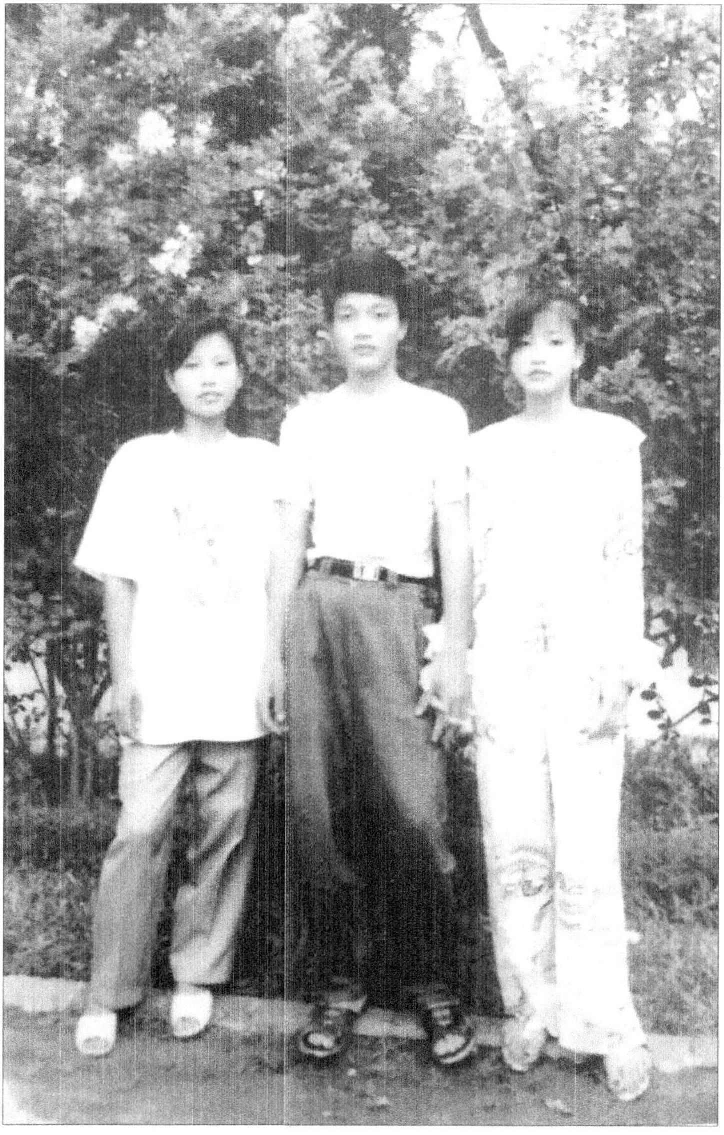

fried pigeon. These were all considered good food to eat with beer. It was a far cry from the slop I had to sell at the station. In the area around the restaurant were many factories and a university, so we were very busy at lunch and dinner time with a constant flow of customers.

In this new environment there were certain differences to working around the station. For a start nobody here swore. Also, I was appreciated for the work I did and this was reflected in my wage. After only a few months I received a pay rise to 250,000 đồng a month (around £17), over double my initial rate. I didn't tell my adoptive mother about this pay rise though as I felt that I was deserving of some treats for all my efforts. The first treat was a good daily breakfast, the second was to have some clothes made.

I quickly realised though that the trouble with this arrangement was that the first time I washed anything new at home it would be at least two weeks before I got to wear it again, as one of my adoptive sisters was now my size and she would take anything new for herself – even my underwear. In fact, even the other daughters who weren't my size would help themselves to my clothes whenever they wanted to, because they could. This was a real frustration for me as by now I was 16 years of age and felt that I should at least have my own things.

The other problem with turning up at the house wearing better clothing was that the family started to look at me differently, and it didn't take long before my adoptive mother started asking to borrow money. I felt obliged to always give her what I could, but I knew that the family thought I had more money than I actually did. It was difficult, and was a tricky situation to navigate.

As I was tired of having any good clothes taken from me, I started to pay for them to be washed near my place of work – and kept my new clothes at the restaurant. This small act was so significant for me because it represented the first time in my life that I could truly call anything my own. Previously things were given to me and taken from me at others behest. I had no control.

At work I could use a nearby public shower that had both cold and hot water on tap – something I'd never had access to before. I was spending more and more time at the restaurant, especially because everybody there was nice to me. I even started to get tips from regular customers. In fact I always seemed to get the most tips of anyone who worked there.

My mornings started on the back of a xe lam, normally shared with people taking their stock to market. Some days it would be chickens, sometimes young pigs. It was always busy on the xe lam as we clucked or grunted our way along the road, and I always tried to sit near the back (where you jumped on and off) as my journey was short. I didn't want to get stuck behind a load of pigs in my smart work clothes after all.

I was at the restaurant for about 18 months or so and it was there that I evolved from a child to a young woman. As well as my new clothes I started to benefit in other areas from the routine of going to work and getting paid regularly. I ate better – often customers wouldn't eat all of their food so there were nutritious scraps to be had. My confidence grew and people started to treat me better. I was no longer the country bumpkin.

I felt like a parched tree in a desert that had finally had a drink of water.

I started to be noticed by men of all types, including by some young men in the area. Sometimes they would call out when I walked past, trying to attract my attention. It was the first time that anyone had wanted to get to know me in this way. The best thing about it was that nobody who saw me now could guess my past. I looked better – I was both well fed and better dressed. People now seemed to want to know me as I was, or rather as I appeared – I still kept my private life to myself and as part of this always told people that I worked for my 'aunt'. I was always very careful not to give people the opportunity to bully me, so letting people know I had a legitimate connection to the area by working for a relative was to my benefit. I was still very aware of my innocence of the world, and bitter experience had taught me that innocence could make you vulnerable. I knew that had people, men especially, been aware of my true position I would have been less secure.

Students Call

One day a group of five young men, perhaps seven or eight years older than me, arrived at the restaurant on motorbikes. I was chosen to serve them and I noticed that one in the group kept looking at me. Over the next week or so he returned several times, only on these occasions he was on his own. He was always smartly dressed and always wanted to talk with me. He told my 'aunt' (the restaurant owner) he was a part-time student, and his name was Toàn. I was happy that such an apparently wealthy and educated person seemed to like me. One day he asked my 'aunt' if I could be allowed to finish early and

go with him to his friend's birthday party (a friend who had been in the initial group when they first came to the restaurant). My 'aunt' asked me if I wanted to go, and I said yes. I changed into my smart clothes and asked him to pick me up near my home as I needed to borrow some nicer shoes to wear. I raced home to change my shoes and waited for Toàn to arrive. He pulled up on a motorbike and I jumped on to the back feeling very nervous. This was the first time I'd ever been out with somebody, and I was doing so on the back of his motorbike riding to his friend's party — another first for me.
The party was in a nightclub – the Queen Bee – and I was The party was in a nightclub – the Queen Bee – and I was relieved to see that all of Toàn's friends seemed to have partners. This meant I could blend into the crowd and not feel so conspicuous. It also meant that there were girls there for me to talk with. I didn't know this at the time, but the club was very luxurious – the smartest such venue in Hà Nội at the time – and I was very happy to have been invited to such a smart place.

At about 10pm I felt that it was getting late and I asked my date if I could go home. His friends said that the party had just started – and would go on until 2 or 3am. I was very nervous, but the boy reassured me it was okay and everybody was happy. Everybody else seemed to be having a good time, and lots of people were dancing. I had never danced but when the lights dimmed and the music changed to a slow number he insisted I dance with him and pulled me on to the dance floor. I told him I couldn't dance and at first was frozen solid. But eventually I decided to at least try, and started moving my feet to the left and right – a bit like a duck waddling. It was my first dance.

When the party finished the group went outside and started to talk about getting something to eat. As my date was my ride home I had no choice but to follow and so we all rode off in search of somewhere open. By now it was very late and when we finished eating I asked again to be taken home. But the others in the group simply asked why I didn't wait until the morning as it was surely too late now to return home. They said it would be worse for me because I would wake the family. They all agreed to take me home in the morning and explain to my adoptive parents why I hadn't returned the night before.

I reluctantly agreed to their logic and three of the five couples then started to roam around the city by motorbike taking in the popular sights – West Lake, Hoàn Kiếm Lake, etc. I remember at this time of the morning it was a bit chilly, and Toàn asked me to wrap my arms around him as we rode along. He knew that I was worried about being out so late. In my head were so many thoughts – but most of all I was fearful that I'd maybe put myself in danger. Perhaps I was with a group of young people like the pleasure-seekers I would often see at the station in the early hours. I feared what I would have to say to my adoptive parents, and what they would think of me for being out so late. But it seemed that nobody was listening to me whenever I tried to press for a lift home.

Eventually one of the other couples suggested that they had been everywhere so why not now find somewhere to stay until morning. They said that they had a friend who might let them stay. So we were off again, eventually pulling up at what looked to be either a large guest house or hotel. It certainly didn't look like a family home. I refused to go in with Toàn and the others and I started to argue with my date. By now I was both upset and frustrated. But this turned to fear when, as we were still parked on the roadside, two men who had roared past us on a large motorcycle stopped after seeing us and turned their machine around. I could tell they were đầu gấu gangsters by the clothes they wore. The fact that they had such an expensive motorbike was a bad sign.

After pulling up alongside us they demanded to know what we were doing. The others in the group explained that we were looking for somewhere to stay before we returned home, and that we'd been to a birthday party. The boys reassured the đầu gấu that the girls were girlfriends, not prostitutes. I was frozen with fear when I watched Toàn talking to them.

One of the two gangsters beckoned me to him and told me to sit on their bike. The rider had the engine running, and the second man forcibly pulled me to them, insisting that I sit in the middle, between them. I froze again when the rider referred to him by name, as I knew it was the name of the city's most dangerous gangster at that time. I was terrified and was desperately shouting 'no' – pleading with the group I was with to help me. I knew I was in trouble and begged them, anyone, to help. I pleaded with the đầu gấu to let me go in peace, but the main gangster pulled out a revolver.

I could see the dread on the faces of the group as they watched events unfolding, mirroring the fear in my own eyes. The gun meant that things were of a different order, and marked the two out as the heavyweight gangsters they were. The main đầu gấu was now angry and he got off the motorbike, took off his helmet – which was military surplus and made of steel – and started to smash it into the boys in the group. They had been pleading with the two to let me go. The motorbike rider then turned to me and asked who my 'leader' was. I presume he thought I was with another group of đầu gấu, but I insisted I wasn't. I told them where I lived – my address, who my adoptive parents were, who my siblings were. I wanted them to know I wasn't a prostitute, and had people who would be looking for me. I carried on begging him to let me go.

The gangster with the gun then walked over to my friend's motorbike and kicked it over. But as he was momentarily distracted doing this I seized on an opportunity to escape, pulled myself away from the motorcycle rider and sprinted towards the guest house we had parked outside. There was a huge iron gate, and I have no idea how I managed to do it but I somehow scrambled up it and jumped over to the other side. I knew that if I had gone with the two it would have been hell, with the worst consequences imaginable. I reached the building and continued to climb, without fear of falling, until I eventually made it all the way to the roof. I thought I was safe but the gangster with the gun held it to Toàn's head and shouted that he would shoot unless I returned. The group begged me to return – screaming that otherwise their friend would surely be shot. But the fear that had gripped me prevented me from moving. I froze, unsure what my next move would be.

A dog's barking eventually alerted the owner of the guest house, who appeared and demanded to know what was going on. He told me to climb down and said I had to leave his property. He said that if I didn't come down he would let the others come in to get me. And so then I knew I had no choice. I climbed down the front of the building and out through the gate, which had been opened by the owner. I walked slowly towards the gangsters' motorbike. By now I was screaming and crying and begging anybody to help. But as I reached the motorbike I knew that in the blink of an eye I would be gone. I screamed and screamed and the gangster with the gun said that if I didn't keep quiet he would start shooting. But I couldn't, didn't, stop.

Out of the blue I heard a loudspeaker – ordering everyone to stay still and raise their hands. It was the police. I pulled myself away from the motorbike and ran to Toàn, and watched as the gangsters were questioned by the officers. I couldn't hear what they were saying, but the police were clearly telling them to leave. I watched as they clicked their bike into gear and rode off down the road. We took our chance and rode off in the opposite direction, once the police were satisfied with our side of the story, hoping all the while that we didn't run in to the two đầu gấu. As we rode along, the group kept apologising to me. But I refused their apologies and demanded to be taken home. Toàn kept saying sorry to me as we rode, and said he had no idea how it could have happened.

The group dropped me close to my house and after a short walk down the alleyway I reached the front door, calling out for my adoptive mother to open it. It must have been about 4.30am and she had to wake up to let me in. She wasn't angry, and I did my best to hide my fear. As soon as I was let in I ran to lay down in the middle of the children, who were fast asleep. For once, they made me feel safe.

The next day I awoke late, and my adoptive mother asked me where I had been. I told her a version of events, failing to mention the đầu gấu and the traumas I had suffered. I also told her a lie – that I had a day off and didn't have to work as the restaurant was closed that day. The fact was I was terrified of being out alone by myself in case the same thing happened again.

From that day on I was always most afraid of being kidnapped. The thought never left my mind – especially if I was out after dark. At the time kidnapping was a real concern, with victims often being forced into prostitution. There were many stories of how even working young women had been kidnapped in this way, and become victims of sex trafficking. It was especially dangerous for vulnerable young women.

I called the restaurant owner on a telephone to say that I was ill and would need a few days to recover. She wasn't happy at all, but I just couldn't face going into work. I had to take the risk that the owner wouldn't fire me. A few days later when I eventually returned to the restaurant I was still plagued by terrible thoughts: why exactly had the gangsters picked on me and not the other girls? Why had they wanted to kidnap me and not them?

The restaurant owner, my 'aunt', told me that the boy who had taken me to the party had called and asked to meet me, and had asked for my address. She said that she hadn't given it to him as it was my business. A few days later Toàn turned up at the restaurant and said he just wanted to know I was okay. He continued to call regularly and after a few such visits he asked me to again go out with him. Still traumatised by what had happened, I refused.

Time passed and he would often come to the restaurant, each time making sure he spoke with me. He would always offer to take me home after work. Eventually I accepted his offer and once again climbed on to the back of his motorbike, and we rode through the evening traffic towards my home. I was careful to ask him to drop me off before we got close to the family's house though, so that he didn't know exactly where my house was – and my adoptive family didn't discover that I knew somebody who had enough money to ride a motorbike.

Toàn did this many times and slowly my confidence in him began to grow. I was a bit overwhelmed by his attention, although I felt ashamed that I was beginning to have feelings for him. Sometimes we would even go for a roam around the city on his motorbike, joining the flow of traffic as it snaked its way into the city centre. It didn't really matter where we rode, be it around Hoàn Kiếm Lake or maybe through the Old Quarter, the important thing was that it was just the two of us together. It was our time.

On one occasion Toàn held my hand as we rode, and seemed to want to show that he cared for me. I felt he respected me. I always told him that I didn't want to stay out for long, and now – after the incident with the đầu gấu – he always took me home when I asked. I started to feel happy that he would meet me after work, and started to wish that he would come a bit sooner so that we could spend more time together.

One day Toàn asked me to go and sing karaoke with him. It was becoming really popular in Việt Nam and I was quite excited at the prospect. I was careful to assure him that I couldn't sing, although he said that I didn't have to as I could listen to somebody else sing – and that person would be him. He intrigued me. I now wanted to know how he sang.

On the chosen day I asked my aunt if I could take an hour off to go to the local karaoke bar. I remember it was 5,000 đồng for an hour, and I remember that to my surprise he could sing very well. After listening for a while Toàn tried to pass me the microphone, which I politely declined. He started to sing a song directly to me and stood up as he sang. He didn't take his eyes off me and I could tell that he knew the words by heart. The song had lines like 'if you come to me please love me with all your heart'. I was shocked and was full of joy at the thought these words were directed at me.

So gradually I started to spend more time with him; we would travel further around the city, return home later. Eventually I was confident enough to show him the alleyway where I lived and confided in him that I lived with adoptive parents. By this time I felt that I could trust him enough to expose this vulnerability.

One day he took me to a garden café on what was then the outskirts of the city. It was a known romantic destination where young couples would meet. When we walked into the garden I could see couples making out. I told Toàn that I didn't feel comfortable, but he started to try and kiss me and hug me regardless. I didn't like this at all and he could tell I felt uncomfortable in this public space, where other people could see us. He then took me to a nearby guest house and said we could have some privacy there. He insisted to me that this is what people who loved each other did, and I believed him. Looking back now I know that I was completely naïve at this point. I simply didn't know what couples did in such situations, so I trusted him that he knew what we should do. The fact is he had drawn me into his world. He was educated and worldly wise and older than me – by seven years. I thought then that he would lead me to a better life. I thought he could fill in the gaps I had.

The guest house had a bed in it, and it was here that I slept with somebody for the first time.

From that point on he would sometimes book a guest house for us to be together, although never overnight. We never again went to a garden café.

The White Cloud

Toàn was a student of the Foreign Trade University and studied part-time. One day he took me to see a shop and said that he had rented it and planned to open a karaoke bar of his own. The bar was quite close to my house – on Lê Duẩn, one of the biggest roads in Hà Nội. He asked me to work with him, making drinks and generally helping run the bar. Toàn was kind and supportive – I would even say he loved me at this point. My starting salary was 1,000,000 đồng a month – a huge amount for me at the time and a big increase from my job at the restaurant. The karaoke bar, which he called Mây Trắng (White Cloud), was luxurious and far more exclusive than almost all other such city-centre venues. At the White Cloud, rather than the usual 5,000 đồng for an hour's karaoke, it was 5,000 đồng for just one song.

Toàn taught me how to mix drinks and pour wine. The main room was big enough for 20 people to sit in and groups would take it in turns to sing – perhaps three or four songs at a time. All the guests knew that I was the owner's girlfriend, so I was treated with respect and they referred to me in a friendly way as cô chủ nhỏ (small owner). By this time my adoptive parents knew that I had a boyfriend who owned a karaoke bar.

One weekend Toàn invited me to have dinner at his house because two of his brothers and a sister were visiting his mother's home. I had already met these three siblings as they had all visited the karaoke bar, although I was yet to meet his mother. By inviting me to formally meet his family things between us seemed to be getting much more serious.

When we arrived, the other guests were already there and I asked my boyfriend if there was anything I could do to help his mother. Straight away I was asked to help prepare the table for the guests. When we sat down for our meal I wasn't allowed to sit next to Toàn, and I felt a bit nervous because of this. Toàn's older sister commented that I was so young to be living together with somebody. His elder brother seemed quite distant. The family seemed to be happy though, they laughed often and conversation between them flowed easily.

It was the first time in my life that I learned weekends were times when people met their families. Toàn's brothers and sisters all had good jobs: one was a teacher, one worked at the central post office, one worked in freight, and one worked in Germany. In other words they were at the exact opposite end of the spectrum to myself and my own background. As if I wasn't nervous enough already.

Toàn's family looked at me inquisitively throughout the meal, although I felt they were generally friendly. I was so nervous I couldn't even reach over to take some food. I was simply shaking too much. I tried to catch Toàn's attention and silently called for help. Everybody asked why I only looked at the food and some of his siblings took it upon themselves and put some food into my bowl. Of course they knew how nervous I was – they could probably see the beads of sweat running down my face. I had never been in a situation where people were insisting I ate. Eventually somebody asked what my parents did. I told them the area where we lived, and said that my mother sold food. There were no more questions[17].

When the meal had finished I volunteered to wash the dishes. This was something I knew how to do. As I was working, his mother came into the kitchen and looked at me. Initially she said nothing, but eventually told me to stand aside to let her take over. She said that my method of washing wasted too much water. So I did as she said, and went to search for Toàn. I told him what his mum had said and he said that she did that with everybody, and not to worry. He reassured me that even when he tried to sweep the floor she would tell him to stop as he wasn't doing it properly.

When we left his parents' house we returned to the karaoke bar to work. By now it had become a great success and had developed a good reputation in Hà Nội. At the time there were very few quality karaoke bars in the city. The location made it easy for people to find and we got busier and busier as each week went by. We would often both join in with the singing, and the atmosphere in the karaoke bar was always good.

---

[17] In Việt Nam it is considered vital that you marry somebody of generally equal status, and certainly from a good family. This is one of the reasons why I was so nervous in this and other social settings. I felt as though I was only ever one question away from being exposed as being somebody with a background and family to be ashamed of.

Toàn's main job was to take customers' song lists, which he would pass to his cousin to play the songs. He would also prepare the bills for customers, while my main job was preparing and serving the drinks. We were open from 11am to 10.30pm – although we rarely closed on time. I would normally return home at around 11.30pm, and this was normally before Toàn had finished. He slept at the bar, along with his cousin. Mornings involved cleaning up from the night before.

I felt comfortable and confident in my new life. I was proud of the way people treated me, and I enjoyed the times I had together with Toàn. We grew together as the bar grew. He was very confident and was very good at talking to people. He made guests feel very welcome.

We would often have celebrities visiting. I had little idea who they were as I seldom watched the TV. But he seemed to know them all and would point out who was who. I can remember the day Thanh Thanh Hiền arrived. She was an actor, singer and comedian so famous that even I had heard of her. What a treat – to hear such a great singer in our bar.

I had now put my heart and soul into both this business and our relationship.

As time passed by and the bar became more and more successful I noticed that I stayed at the same wage. Although this was much higher than in my previous job, it was normal in a successful business that your wages reflected this fact. I would normally have expected a wage rise after a few months. In truth, oftentimes I wouldn't even receive my pay. But I didn't mind. I was thinking only that we were now a couple.

Now that I was confident with Toàn I asked him to come with me to visit my grandmother and uncle, and some days later we set out early to ride to the village I was so fond of. Once again I stopped at the garden gate and called out to see who was home, only this time it was with my partner. My uncle and grandmother were very happy when we arrived, and especially when they realised I had a good job and that Toàn seemed reliable. After lunch we returned to Hà Nội, but not before he had given my grandmother a sum of money. I was so impressed and touched by this – an act which you would only expect from somebody truly committed to me. On the journey back to Hà Nội I held him as tightly as possible – in an effort to show him how I felt.

A wedding or two

One day, on my way to work, my adoptive mother told me that the eldest daughter was getting married and that she wanted a loan from me. I said that I didn't have any spare money, but she asked why I wouldn't ask Toàn. She promised to return the money as soon as the wedding ceremony was over. She asked for 3,000,000 đồng. I said that was a lot, but she reassured me that once the guest 'envelopes'[18] were collected she would repay the loan in full.

That day my legs were heavy as I walked to work, wondering how I could ask Toàn, as I didn't have anywhere near that amount money saved. I told Toàn what had happened and asked him to give me the money I needed. He agreed, but at the same

---

[18] Guests at weddings are expected to give the bride and groom some money towards the day, handed over in gift envelopes.

time didn't seem happy about it, and our ride to my house that afternoon was silent. This was the first time I had taken him to the house, but I wanted my adoptive parents to know that they were borrowing his money, not mine.

Toàn stayed for only around ten minutes and it was agony for me: here was a huge part of my life being exposed to the person I loved in front of my eyes and there was nothing I could do about it. It was inevitable, and it was unavoidable, but inside I was screaming – wanting to know what he thought of my adoptive parents. All I could do was to see how he reacted to them. The reality was, given how much older he was than me, he was probably aware of the kind of people they were, and the kind of life they led. To me, he gave nothing away though.

By this time the Tết celebrations had passed and we had been together for over a year. Toàn bought me a second-hand bicycle from his brother for me to use, and give me some independence. It also helped him because it meant that he didn't have to drop me home of an evening. The bicycle was Japanese and of very good quality – a rarity in Việt Nam at that time[19].

Between the karaoke bar and my home I rode on my new bicycle past my former life – past the street sellers hawking their goods, past the pickpockets and the children hanging around with little to do. It seemed that I had moved on. Each morning I would wake up my boyfriend and his cousin when I arrived at

---

[19] At this time in Việt Nam few people had motorbikes and most rode around on cheap Chinese, or Vietnamese, bicycles. The wealthy though rode imported bicycles, and the finest of these were from Japan. The machines were of much higher quality, and were so much smoother and more reliable than the cheaper bicycles.

the bar. They slept there overnight – on the sofas used by customers. We would clean and make it fresh. Around lunchtime we would go for cơm bình dân (fast food for working people) in the area. Of an evening, we would go for dinner independently as we always had customers by then and at least one of us had to remain in the bar. Even if we still had customers, by 11.30pm I could go home.

My life seemed perfect at this time.

Two months went by, the daughter was married, and my adoptive parents asked again to borrow money because this time their son was getting married. Of course, they had yet to pay back the money from their daughter's wedding, but it didn't stop them from asking. I was so sad and ashamed to have to ask Toàn again, and held the news in for as long as I could. But eventually I felt I had no alternative but to again ask him. I hadn't told him yet what my adoptive parents had told me – that at the first wedding the envelopes guests had given were too 'small', i.e. hadn't contained enough money for them to repay the loan. I felt that I hadn't needed to tell him because the money had really belonged to me – it was effectively unpaid wages. In fairness, Toàn had never asked for the money back. But it was nevertheless a terrible experience for me to have to ask for another loan.

My solution was to ask Toàn for just 1,000,000 đồng so that I could give it to the son as a gift, from us both. Toàn agreed and I returned home and gave the money to my adoptive mother. She took it without reply. I felt relief. But three days' later I couldn't find my bicycle. I was told that the oldest daughter had borrowed it. I thought nothing of it and walked to work. But two more days passed and there was still no sign of it.

Toàn asked where my bicycle was and I told him the eldest daughter had borrowed it to help arrange the wedding of her brother. On the day of the wedding I returned to the house for a couple of hours to help. Again there was no sign of my bicycle, and again I asked my adoptive mother where it was. She said she had pawned it. I was frozen. It was my precious bicycle, a bike that had been gifted to me. She said that I would need 500,000 đồng to get it back. I was helpless – I felt I couldn't ask Toàn for another 500,000 đồng. That night I slept at the shop instead of returning home, and eventually told Toàn what had happened. He was shocked. I felt humiliated.

Time went by and over the next few weeks I was sleeping at the karaoke bar rather than returning home. One day I noticed that my period was missing. When I said that I felt something had changed in my body, Toàn took me to see a doctor, who carried out some form of 'internal procedure'. Toàn told the doctor to only tell him what the issue was, rather than me. Toàn later told me the problem was 'menstrual conditioning' and said that we couldn't have a baby at that time. He said there were many reasons.

I felt I had to listen to him and take his advice. Toàn reassured me it was nothing serious and we could sort it out 'gently'. In my naivety I didn't know that I must have been pregnant and had had an early-stage abortion. I had nobody to ask for such information.

Later on he took me home and said that I should take a couple of days off. I lied to my adoptive mother and said that I was unwell and needed to rest. I suspect she noticed what the real issue was, although didn't say anything. In the meantime Toàn had given me some money so that I could at least get my bicycle back.

In the house there had been a slight change while I had been staying at the bar. As previously, all the (unmarried) children slept on grass mats but they were now placed on to a wooden bed, on the first floor. The parents slept on the ground floor, while the married son now slept on the mezzanine with his wife. The married daughter, as is customary in Việt Nam, had moved out and was living with her husband's family.

Occasionally, my adoptive mother would make some crab soup to sell in the alleyway by the house. Along with the money I gave her, this was the family's only source of income. The father still didn't work and by now the children had left school and all were jobless. They were hanging around with drug addicts and various đầu gấu, who sometimes would come into the house. I would always be polite and say 'hello', but wouldn't say anything else to them.

Life returned to some sort of routine. I went to work on my bicycle and the work was the same as before. The only thing that had changed was Toàn, who now seemed to be behaving differently towards me. But when I asked him about it he said that I was just thinking 'silly thoughts'. As more time went on though, it was apparent that he was avoiding me. Sometimes he would send me home early, saying that he would sort the bar out himself.

A stranger calls

At this time I noticed also that sometimes he left the bar, even though we were open for business. On one occasion he said that he had to attend a class as he had started to study again – and needed to show his face at university. He said that up to that point his friends had been writing down his name in the daily register at university to allow him to work. He said that he had an exam approaching and needed to catch up.

By this time I could ride a motorbike, so I offered to drop him off and pick him up later. I felt that I didn't trust what he had told me. He accepted my offer and we rode together to his university. Just before the entrance, however, he jumped off, telling me that motorbikes weren't allowed on campus. So I returned home – and even felt happy that he had let me give him a lift. I headed back to the bar to work and not long later he turned up. I asked why he had turned up early and he said that his friends had made a mistake – and told him the wrong day. But he seemed to be warmer towards me and was showing some affection. I was grateful for this as it seemed we were returning to how things had been.

The next time he said he had to go to university I didn't think much of it, as by now I felt I trusted him again.

Things went on this way for a few weeks until one day I answered a phone call at the bar. When I picked up the phone the caller cut the line. I had a feeling something was not right. Toàn returned the call in the bar and I listened to his conversation. It was all "um, ah" and I could tell he was deliberately not having a conversation with the caller.

Suspicious, I made my way to the landlord's flat upstairs and asked him if I could use his phone to listen in (there was a shared line). Toàn would have known I was listening in but couldn't do anything about it. The caller seemed angry and told Toàn he had two faces and that she had changed her mind about going to his nephew's birthday party with him. I hadn't been told of this birthday celebration. When I returned to the bar Toàn shouted at me. He said I had showed him no respect by listening to his private conversation. He said that the caller was a friend from university and there was nothing between them. He said that I could never again listen to him. I was so angry – but the hurt and betrayal I felt choked my voice. Around 7pm he left and I asked his cousin if he knew where Toàn was going. He said that he was going to the party. I felt hurt that he hadn't invited me.

The next day I turned up to work as normal but Toàn was clearly avoiding having a conversation with me. When I returned home to eat my lunch my adoptive mother asked if she could borrow my bicycle for ten minutes, and of course I had to agree. But after 15 minutes she hadn't returned so I had to walk back to the bar.

By now the happy atmosphere that we had previously was gone. I said that I wanted to go home early – partly out of anger with him, and partly to find out where my bicycle was. Toàn didn't offer to take me home, so I walked. In my head were so many questions. When I arrived at the house there was no sign of my bicycle – and I knew instantly what had happened[20]. My

---

[20] This was the second of many times my adoptive mother was to pawn my bicycle without paying for its return.

adoptive mother said she had pawned it again to repay a debt, and she said she had borrowed just 200,000 đồng and had a month to repay it. Inside I was in turmoil.

For the next few days I walked to and from the bar. Toàn was hardly speaking to me. It was clear that we had a big problem, and it was clear now that he had been having a relationship with the girl on the phone. I felt as though he didn't need me anymore, and didn't even need me to work at the bar. That evening I asked Toàn to give me a ride home – to give me the opportunity to ask him some questions. When we were near my home I asked him for some money so that I could at least retrieve my bicycle once more – so that I didn't have to ask for a lift.

The next morning I went to the public phone box and called the bar. His cousin answered and I told him that I wasn't well and needed a few days off. I said that I was so angry and jealous and couldn't work.

But after three days, and Toàn still hadn't come to see how I was, I returned to work regardless. Toàn's cousin seemed pleased to see me, but the same wasn't true for Toàn. It was painful for me but I managed to stay at the bar, working until the early evening. Eventually I said to Toàn that if I wasn't needed then I wouldn't turn up for work the next day. He seemed awkward and mumbled that it was "up to me". So the next day I stayed at home to let him know that I meant what I said, and was very upset.

In my heart I hoped that he would come to find me and make things better, but day turned into week and then a month had gone by and he had still not turned up at my house. In the end I called the bar, but whenever I did the cousin said that Toàn was busy and couldn't talk.

In desperation I eventually went back to the bar to see him. Toàn was polite but extremely cold. Despite this, for some reason, I still felt that we could patch things up if only we had the opportunity to discuss the situation. So over the next few weeks I would occasionally visit the bar in the hope that Toàn would talk with me – hoping that if I turned up at different times of day we would at least have the opportunity to speak. I just couldn't accept that the relationship we'd had seemed to have disappeared so completely. The relationship had been my security. The one thing I'd never had. We had run a business together, almost had a child together. We had met each other's families. We'd been like husband and wife, and I had trusted him enough to expose my vulnerabilities. I felt so betrayed.

Although I knew I wasn't really welcome anymore at the White Cloud, one evening I turned up there late – at around 9pm. Toàn said that I should return home because he was working. He told me not to return again. I felt ashamed that he had rejected me in this way, rejecting me so boldly and openly – and it was a pain that wouldn't go away. His words stripped away my very being, and left me feeling that I was worthless – just as I had been made to feel for my whole life. It was the disrespect that hurt so much – the fact that he hadn't even had the decency to sit down and have a conversation about it, preferring instead to just brush me off by telling me to go so casually. I felt that if Toàn, the person who knew me better than anybody else, didn't want me then surely nobody would. My situation seemed even more hopeless because, up to this point, I felt Toàn was the one person who could understand me – and, more than this, I knew also that people in the local area knew that I had been part of a couple. In a society like Việt Nam's, so governed by social mores and attitudes, my humiliation in everybody's eyes would be complete.

The relationship with Toàn, and the security I had felt within it, had given me a confidence I'd never had before. But now that confidence had gone – it was replaced with an abyss of self-doubt. It sent me into a crushing spiral – to the point that I didn't want to live anymore.

The reality of my situation now really sank in – and I felt that I had no chance in life from this point on. Rejected in the manner in which I had been, as well as living in the area I did, meant that people would call me a prostitute. I blamed myself for this – and I also blamed my adoptive parents for the trouble they had caused and the loans they had asked from Toàn. Perhaps he had feared that by staying with me my adoptive family would just cause more and more trouble for him, and for his own family.

More days went by and in desperation I returned to the bar and asked to stay overnight. I thought this would force him to speak with me. But he insisted on taking me home. On the way home I demanded to know why he had acted in the way he had. Eventually he said that some of his friends had seen me sitting on the back of another man's motorbike. He was accusing me of being unfaithful with him. I promised that I hadn't done this but he called me a liar and told me to leave him alone. He, once again, asked me to never return to the bar.

I was devastated when he dropped me off and left on his motorbike. Inside I was destroyed, crying to myself while standing in a corner of the alleyway. In my pain, the following lyrics of a song wouldn't leave me: 'In my head the words resounded. The boy who had given me a sweet wound without any debt, let our love fly high'. In my bag I had already collected 100 sleeping tablets – it had taken me a few days to buy them. I returned home and, after making sure there was some money in my drawer for the family to use[21] once I was gone, and with the family sleeping, I swallowed them all.

The morning after I had returned home, my adoptive siblings apparently wondered why I hadn't come down for lunch. One of them checked on me and saw that I was soaking wet with sweat, and frothing around my mouth. The family took me to hospital and I was kept there for a couple of days.

Over the next few days, as I slowly recovered, the pain of my situation returned to me in waves. I was like a zombie – completely washed out and obsessively going over Toàn's rejection. When my adoptive mother told me that Toàn's cousin and his friend had come to visit the hospital to see how I was, it served only to make the sense of rejection worse.

It took a long time until I felt that I was starting to recover from the ordeal. But when I felt strong enough – both physically and emotionally – I decided that I had to go again to the White Cloud to see the person who had brought me to the point where I had wanted to end my life. I felt that I just couldn't let things

---

[21] I had left 500,000 đồng.

end in the way they had. I decided this time not to enter the bar, but rather just to stand outside. I needed to see him.

But instead of Toàn, it was his cousin who eventually came outside to talk with me and exchange a few words. I realised that it had been a pointless mission – Toàn had no intention of ever seeing me again, so I said goodbye to the cousin and left.

As I walked along the street and made my way home I could hear people whispering that I was "thất tình" (crazy with love). I knew then that no matter what I did now, or even in the future, this is how I would be known in this community. Of course there was nobody I could share this pain with. So I gritted my teeth, and as I did finally realised that in order to survive I had to try and build another life. This time for myself.

Time for a change

So I started by looking for another job, this time in a different neighbourhood. Quite quickly I found one, working in a restaurant as a waitress. Although it wasn't an especially good place to work it was at least something different. It was a start. It also gave me a new window on to the world, and an opportunity to meet new people. With my first month's wage I bought a nice pair of shoes and a new dress, just to lift my spirits.

Through the steady stream of customers at the restaurant I met some good people, and one day one of them told me of a much better job opportunity at a different restaurant, where she worked. As I was still determined to make for myself a new and better life, I decided to go along and enquire. After all, I'd been working at the restaurant for four to five months by this time. The role was for a marketing girl and the restaurant was clearly a step up from the one where I was working at the time. I was to be employed to promote Tiger Beer, which was the biggest beer company in Việt Nam.

During this time I felt that I was starting to rebuild my life and I had finally accepted that in order to do so I would have to leave all thoughts of Toàn behind. I told myself that somebody from my social background could not hope to marry someone from Toàn's. This wasn't the way things happened in Việt Nam. It was a sadness I would just have to bear.

I reminded myself that I had met good people – especially those I was meeting lately at the restaurant. These new people were helping to lift my confidence. But I was also slowly becoming aware that although this was partly genuine altruism on their part, it was also in their interest. I was young and it was clear that other people thought I was attractive and, as such, was a 'good person to know'. I was okay with this knowledge, as it meant that I had some social agency. I determined that I would no longer allow anybody to hurt me again. I also made a conscious effort to be 'lighter' and less serious – I wanted to enjoy interacting and joking at work with my colleagues and the customers.

Now, in my new job, I was handing over 300,000 đồng a month to my adoptive family. I asked a friend's mother to hold the remainder of my wage as I didn't want my adoptive mother to take it.

In Việt Nam there is a big culture of tipping service staff. As this new restaurant had karaoke rooms and was very popular, my tips were really good. Most of the customers were professional and relatively well-to-do. Lots of valuable contracts were agreed over meals at the restaurant – and, often, whenever there were large amounts of money involved in a deal the tips would be particularly large.

One regular customer who was very quiet and polite would always give me a tip whenever he came to the restaurant with some of his friends or clients. He would slip money into my hand on his way out and was my most regular tipper. I never knew what to say. One time he asked me to speak privately with him. He had booked a separate dining room for himself and his friends, and outside the room he put his hand into his pocket and pulled some paper out, before pressing it into my hand. He said that he just wanted to help me. I bowed my head and said thank you and he slipped into the room to join his friends.

When I looked at the piece of paper I didn't recognise what it was, so I asked my manager for help. He looked at me, shocked. My manager said that it was a note that was the biggest denomination in Việt Nam at the time, and wasn't like normal currency. He said that I needed to take it to a gold shop or a bank to change it into smaller notes. He said that the paper was worth a staggering 5,000,000 đồng.

I was mortified in case this huge amount of money came with 'strings' – expectations on the part of the customer. My manager may have thought similarly because he asked why he had given me this. I explained that he had simply pressed it into my hand. At that time 5,000,000 đồng was worth about $500 – an unimaginable amount of money for somebody in my situation.

I could hardly wait to take the certificate to the gold shop to see if this dream was real. The man in the gold shop looked me up and down suspiciously when I presented it, but didn't say anything. I asked straight away what it was worth, and he confirmed that it was indeed 5,000,000 đồng. I asked if it would be possible to change it into dollars. He nodded, left the counter for a short while, and returned with my money. With commission it was a little under $500. The dream was real after all.

I couldn't believe that I had this amount of money in my hand, but I knew that there were dangers attached to it. Chief among them were the risk that my adoptive parents would want it, so I decided to leave all of the money with my friend's mother and not mention it to anybody else. I explained to my friend's mother that I was saving up to buy a motorbike, and told her that a kind customer had given me this amount to help me buy one quicker.

Wheels of my own

After several more months I had enough money saved to buy my first motorbike. I guess it took me about a year in total to have enough for a second-hand machine. I asked my friend's mother to keep an eye out for anybody selling a good one. One day she said that she knew of a good deal – although the asking price was a bit more than I could afford. In Việt Nam at the time, and to an extent even today, people rarely used banks. If you needed a loan it was common to ask family or friends to help. So I asked a few of my friends to chip in and lend me the extra I needed. They agreed and I finally had enough to buy it. I was so excited.

When I returned home on my new, second-hand, motorbike my adoptive parents were shocked. They asked if it was my bike and I explained that I had borrowed money from friends to buy it. I knew that they wouldn't believe me, and I knew that they would think I had turned to prostitution to be able to afford this. In the area where I lived, this was about the only way somebody in my position could hope to afford their own motorbike. But I couldn't let them think that I had enough money for such an expensive thing, so assured them that I had borrowed the money.

Although I was slightly apprehensive about bringing it home, I was confident that a motorbike was too big a thing to be pawned – even for my adoptive parents.

The first person I visited on my bike was my grandmother. For safety, I asked a friend to accompany me. It was a journey of around 60 kilometres and as we rode along I couldn't help reflecting on how happy I was with this new-found mobility. Best of all, I knew that with my motorbike I would be able to visit her whenever I wanted to.

When I returned home my adoptive mother asked when I would visit my father in my home village. I said that I didn't know.

About a week later I awoke in a strange state – like a sleep paralysis. I felt like I'd been drugged. I knew I had to get up and go to work but I was physically incapable of moving. I was frozen and my limbs wouldn't work. After struggling for a long time I somehow managed to force myself to get out of bed, but when I looked at the clock I saw that it was already past lunchtime – hours after I would ordinarily have been up. I knew that something was not right – and clutched my chest to check my motorbike key. I always kept it inside my bra – as close to me as possible. It had gone. I crawled off my sleeping mat and staggered downstairs, holding the wall and anything else I could grip to stop me from falling. When I reached the bottom of the stairs I looked to see if my bike was there, but it had gone. I froze – and staggered outside, asking anybody I met if they had seen my adoptive mother. My heart was pounding. I felt dizzy with nausea. My precious motorbike had gone.

The shock of this started to bring me around though, and could feel the strength returning to my legs. As fast as I could manage I walked around the neighbourhood in a blind panic, desperately looking for some sign that my motorbike was still around, before eventually returning home when I realised there was none. By now my adoptive father was sat in the downstairs room, and I asked him where my motorbike was. He reassured me that my adoptive mother had simply borrowed it and would soon return. So I sat upstairs and waited. I was panicking and crying but I knew that there was nothing I could do.

After what seemed like an age I heard my adoptive mother return, and I ran downstairs to demand to know what she had done with my motorbike, which was nowhere to be seen. She said simply that she had pawned it, but wouldn't tell me where or for how much. I was distraught and flew upstairs, again in tears.

At dinner time nobody in the family asked me to join them to eat. From upstairs I could hear that once dinner was finished, the family all went outside. I was alone in the house.

Later that evening the son-in-law arrived. He asked where everybody else was and I explained that they had gone out after dinner. He was an addict and đầu gấu, and most of his friends were the same. I'd purposefully never had a conversation with him, but this time I couldn't avoid one. He asked me to go out with him – promising to introduce me to a friend of his, who he claimed could give me a good job with opportunities. I knew that he was a threat and as we were alone together I was vulnerable. I told him that I already had a job, and when the opportunity arose I made my way to the front door and slipped out of the house. Once in the alleyway I felt safe. I waited until he had left before returning home.

It took hours for my adoptive mother to return. This time I demanded to know where she had pawned my bike, and why. She explained that the family had needed money to pay for a tribute to their late grandmother[22], and had no alternative. I demanded to know why she hadn't asked me to lend her the money. But all of my questions were met with silence. When my adoptive father returned I begged to know how much they had pawned it for and where it was, but he was similarly silent. My feeling of despair was complete – they weren't even giving me the chance to get my motorbike back. I felt helpless at this point.

But eventually my adoptive mother relented, and said that she had pawned it for 5,000,000 đồng, borrowed over 30 days. She

---

[22] In Việt Nam, at certain set intervals, ancestors must be venerated by conducting acts of tribute to them. The main act is normally conducted either three or five years after the ancestor's death. It involves exhuming the body and gathering all of the bones, which are then washed and placed into a ceramic casket. In so doing the ancestor is believed to be at rest for eternity. Other than the burning of incense and votive offerings, this is the final act in the death rituals.

still wouldn't say where she had pawned it. It felt like my world was collapsing around me, again. I knew now why they hadn't wanted to tell me. This was a huge sum of money. There was nobody I could borrow this amount of from, and so I thought my precious motorbike was gone forever.

In my panic and anxiety, I hadn't eaten all day and I felt faint. I couldn't even swallow the food my adoptive mother had left for me. Instead I went outside to buy some instant noodles. I knew I needed to eat, but couldn't face the family's food. My anger was boiling over. I sat down and forced myself to eat, and once finished decided to continue asking around to see if anybody knew where my motorbike was. What use this would have been I don't know, as the real issue was the out-of-reach 5,000,000 đồng I needed for its return. In any case, nobody I asked seemed to know anything.

Suddenly, I had a thought. I jumped on to a xe ôm (motorbike taxi) and directed the rider to a slum area where the younger sister of my adoptive mother lived. I couldn't remember exactly where it was but I knew the general area, so I guided the motorcyclist to where I thought I wanted to go. It was near Long Biên Bridge, which crossed the Red River, on the river side of the dyke which protected Hà Nội. This area would flood each year when the river level rose and was where many of the city's poorest lived.

When I arrived in the neighbourhood I started to walk around asking people if they knew the woman, my adoptive aunt. Eventually, somebody pointed me in the right direction and I thought I recognised the hut where she lived. Although I'd been there once before some years ago, accompanying my adoptive mother on a trip, I had only the vaguest of memories of the hut. I also knew this was a long-shot, but now I was here I was committed. I went into the hut and saw the woman I was looking for sitting there. I noticed straight away that there was a motorbike in the corner with an old blanket covering it. It had to be mine. The sister looked shocked to see me. I told her that my adoptive mother had sent me to pick up the motorbike. She stared at me, thought for a while, and told me that if I wanted to take it I would have to return with my adoptive mother and 'the money'. There was nothing else I could do at this point, but I now knew at least where my motorbike was.

The next day I returned to work at the restaurant and could think only of how I could get my motorbike back. Instead of just despair I now started to think of ways I could achieve this. I knew that I had made some good friends at the restaurant, and started to wonder if I asked each for a chunk of the money enough might agree and I would have the full amount. It was a long-shot I knew but it was the only way I could think of to get hold of such a large sum. So I plucked up the courage and one by one started to ask my friends.

Mercifully, by the end of the day enough friends had agreed to lend me the money I needed, the full 5,000,000 đồng. It took three days for my friends to raise the money, but eventually I had it all.

My next problem was how to make sure I got my motorbike back. As desperate as I was to reclaim it I didn't trust my adoptive mother to actually help. I said that I would go with her to hand over the money and reclaim it. But she refused. I was so afraid that she would spend the money if I simply passed it over to her. I said that it had been extremely hard for me to borrow this money and I needed the motorbike to sell to repay the 'hot' debt[23].

I persuaded a friend to go to my house and explain that she was the person who had lent me the money. She offered to give my adoptive mother a lift to her sister's hut to collect the motorbike. But again my adoptive mother refused. I knew then I had no option but to hand over this huge sum to my adoptive mother. The thought made me feel sick again. She promised to return with the bike, and so with great trepidation I handed over all of the money that I had borrowed. My adoptive mother left the house. All I could do now was hope.

My friend kindly stayed with me as I waited. I was shaking, although I tried to hide it. I knew what I was going to say to the family if I ever again had the motorbike keys in my hand. The two of us walked around the area as she didn't want to wait inside my house. Although I had sensed my adoptive mother's embarrassment, in my head I had reached a decision. There was no turning back now.

Eventually, to my great relief, my adoptive mother returned with the bike, along with its documents, which had presumably been taken from my hiding place. My friend immediately asked for the documents, and I was given the keys. I had my motorbike at last.

---

[23] Hot debts are those involving money borrowed at extremely high rates of interest, with extreme forfeit for late payment. To this day it is still an extremely common way for people lacking traditional avenues for loans to access relatively large amounts of money.

Now it was time. I took a breath, turned to my adoptive parents and asked them calmly to sit down. With my friend at the door watching on, I told them simply that I wanted to move out, softening the blow by promising to visit occasionally. My adoptive father looked at me and said that I should instead sell the motorbike, pay back my friends, and stay with the family. I said no.

Free as a bird

I turned and left the house, clutching the keys in my hand. Without a backward glance I jumped on my motorbike and, with my friend riding behind me, rode off. We rode and rode, and eventually arrived at the beautiful West Lake. Pulling up on our bikes we sat at the lakeside and ate some sunflower seeds. I felt an unbelievable sense of relief.

My friend had promised that I could stay with her for the short term. Her name was Thư (Letter) and she was a colleague from the restaurant. Thư had a simple room not far from the centre of the city and worked part-time, studying at college the rest of the time. I asked if she would allow me to stay until I could find a place of my own, and Thư kindly agreed. We were best friends at the time – even though I was four years younger. Thư impressed me – by the way she managed to support herself at college by working hard and still stay kind and generous to those around her. I stayed with her for a week or so, before moving out and into the house of a relative, Chú Tụng (Uncle Tung), who lived in Hà Nội, not too far from the restaurant.

I had only recently found out that my uncle and aunt were living in the city through a chance meeting with a soldier who was dining at the restaurant where I was working. During the course of a conversation I told him that I had a relative – my father's first cousin – who also worked for the military, and explained that I knew she was in Hà Nội but didn't know where. He had asked her name and when I gave it to him surprisingly said that he knew her and offered to take me to where she lived. He said it was only a ten-minute journey. Although I was slightly wary of his offer, something told me to trust him and, besides, I thought it would be wonderful to meet another relative. So I asked my manager for a bit of time off, and followed the soldier as he rode through the streets towards, what turned out to be, the very edge of the city.

The man was good to his word and took me directly to my relative's house. Cô Tám (Aunty Eight[24]) lived in a simple, one-room temporary home close to her barracks. The soldier knocked on her door and explained that he had brought her niece to see her. Cô Tám was clearly shocked that I had found her. There were no hugs, not even a hand shake, between us as these would have been considered inappropriate. There was just a glance. But there was a kindness and warmth in her eyes that suggested she was pleased to see me. She told the soldier that I was indeed her relative.

From that point on I had made a connection with family members who lived in Hà Nội. Cô Tám was the sister of Chú Tụng and they both made me feel instantly very welcome. I was beginning to feel less alone.

---

[24] It was very common in those days for parents with many children to call the younger ones by a number. Often this would start at about the fifth child (Năm). My own mother was Number Seven (Bảy).

One day I was visiting a temple in Hà Tây, 20km or so from Hà Nội. This was rare for me because although I would visit a temple every month to honour my ancestors and sometimes pray for their help, the temples would normally be in Hà Nội. But now I was mobile and could go further afield. And besides, the temple at Hà Tây was well known as being especially sacred.

As is usual when entering a temple I stood in front of the altar, clasped my hands together and slowly bowed three times. Other temple-goers brought offerings to place on the altar for their ancestors. I had only a few sticks of incense, which I lit and prayed again for my siblings, wherever they were.

As I moved away from the altar I bumped into a woman, Phương, who had used to work at my current restaurant as a manager. Phương had left for another job at another restaurant and we had always got on well. She was a lot older than me and clearly had a lot of life experience that I didn't have, which I valued.

Without thinking, I jokingly said that if she knew of any vacancies at her restaurant could she let me know. The fact was I had been in the same job for some time now and had been feeling that a change could be a good idea. Phương said that she was now working at a better place, and that she was the manager. It was near Trúc Bạch Lake, next to West Lake, which I knew to be a great location – one of the best in Hà Nội. Phương told me to come to her restaurant sometime and check it out. She said it was a cut above the restaurant where I was working.

So I went along for a visit and from the outset liked the look of the place. It was bigger again than my current restaurant and was far smarter. I knew that this meant the clients would be wealthier and the tips bigger[25]. Phương offered me a job there and then. I was keen to accept. She told me that I would be marketing beer and wine at the restaurant – basically, encouraging customers to drink more. It didn't take a lot – especially when the drinkers were men keen to show off in front of their friends and guests.

There were a few 'tricks of the trade' I quickly learnt. The first and foremost was to always bring more bottles than the customer had requested – to leave on the table. In Việt Nam there is a lot of bravado surrounding drinking, and often men in particular would drink more than they had initially intended as the meal progressed. It was always 'một trăm phàn trăm' (100 per cent, or bottoms up). The second tip was that when men offered me a drink in exchange for them drinking more I would always accept – although I learnt to sip just a little and hold it in my mouth until I had the opportunity to surreptitiously spit it into the tissue that I would always hold in my hand. At the time I neither knew how to, nor wanted to, drink alcohol. But the customers never knew.

Phương had a very strong character and clearly commanded respect in the restaurant. She had been in the military and was used to giving orders, and used to being obeyed. But she was very kind to me and would always introduce me to her regular

---

[25] In Việt Nam it was – and still is – very common for workers to change jobs in the service industries regularly. By doing so is the best way to keep your tips high, because as a new face people – usually men – are keen to impress you.

customers. She would tell me who to pay particular attention to – especially the big drinkers. I think she was working on commission and would receive a good bonus at the end of each month if a lot of alcohol had been sold.

Now, all the experience I'd gained over the many years of selling things came in useful. I knew how to read people, and how to promote particular drinks if they were being targeted for sale by the restaurant – usually the expensive spirits like Remy Martin, Johnny Walker or Hennessey XO, etc, where the profits were greatest. I enjoyed the work, and felt confident in my new environment – making customers feel comfortable. I was very attentive and, though I was paid only a basic wage, I also earned very good tips – always adding up to more than my wage.

As I was a relatively new face among the serving staff, Phương often used me to push certain expensive or exclusive drinks. Of course, if I was asked by customers to bring one bottle to their table, I would always bring two or three, reassuring them that if they didn't drink the bottles they wouldn't have to pay. They usually did though. I felt very relaxed in this job – especially because Phương was my friend, and she was the restaurant manager. I didn't have to fear the jealousy of others, or worry about competing against them for tips. In all I was there for about ten months, and in that time managed to repay all of the money I had borrowed from my friends at the previous restaurant. I was debt free.

Eventually, I decided to move in with my elder sister, Lien, who was renting little more than a shack on the outskirts of the city. I didn't want to outstay my welcome at Chú Tụng's house, and although my new living quarters were extremely basic they were at least somewhere I could call home.

With my new-found freedom, good wages and debts to my friends paid back, I would sometimes visit my adoptive parents. I was always careful to give them some money, as I knew they needed it.

While back in my old neighbourhood I would also take any opportunity to ask around to see if anybody knew what had happened to little Luyến, my baby sister. But every time I was met with the same response: "lâu rồi, không biệt được" (too long ago to remember). Regardless, I urged my adoptive mother to keep asking on my behalf, and reassured her that if anybody could give me any information at all then I would reward them.

The community that lived around the station was very close-knit, and most people knew who I was. I always hoped that somehow my adoptive mother might overhear people talking about Luyến, even if they hadn't wanted to tell me anything directly when I had asked them. The problem was that although it was close-knit, the community was very transient and people would often move on in search of better opportunities. This meant that as time went on there were fewer and fewer people around who could possibly have known anything.

As Bác Hồ Chí Minh famously said "không có gì qúy hơn độc lập tự do" (there is nothing so precious as independence and freedom). I now had a taste of freedom and I could begin to stretch my wings at last. I had my motorbike for transport, and money to give people should I need to. Once a year I would visit my father, but I would visit my grandmother more often. I could make the journey to and from the countryside in one day, as I could only ever hope for an occasional day off work – a few times a year.

I always had a good reception whenever I visited my grandmother, and my uncle and aunt would cook delicious country food. I was proud that I could call them close relatives. They had a nice house and some land and it was a good place to visit.

I would love to ride around the city on my motorbike, too. Everything was still new to me and I began to think that I still had a journey to complete. This meant that I had to start filling in the gaps I felt that I still had in my life, and the most important seemed to be my inability to read. The only lessons I had ever had were the few violent episodes when my father had tried to teach me. But I could remember nothing from these. My problem now was: how to start?

At first I bought myself a newspaper, just to look at it in the hope I could somehow read it like I saw others doing. I started with the smallest story – painfully trying to work out what words might have meant. My only experience of 'reading' had been through my time at the karaoke bar. I would learn songs by heart and try to follow the lyrics on the TV screen as customers sang along. Of course the words were just patterns to me then, I wasn't actually reading. I also used my rides around the city to help me start reading – firstly by recognising street names that I was familiar with: Lê Duẩn, Nguyễn Thái Học and Phố Đình Ngang. I also knew the station name: Ga Hàng Cỏ, on Trần Qúy Cáp Street.

My motorbike was giving me the wings and an opportunity to stretch my mind. I returned to the various markets I frequented as I knew what they were called: Chợ Ngô Sỹ Liên, Chợ Đồng Xuân. I would stand and look at the signs, mouthing the sounds as I scanned my gaze across them. I also looked at menus to recognise words, and I knew drinks from my time at the restaurants and karaoke bar. Bit by bit, I began to piece things together – recognising how words were formed and how combinations of letters sounded.

Even with just a few words my confidence was growing. I pushed myself to learn more and build on these tiny foundations. I felt the power that reading gave people and I knew that I had to take any opportunity that presented itself to expand my knowledge. I started reading shop signs – starting with ones that I knew. On one joyful occasion somebody asked me if I knew an address. They showed me the address written on a piece of paper and I recognised it. I told them how to get there. It was such a small thing, but to me it was a giant step in my development. I was so proud of myself that I had managed to do this. It meant that somebody had looked at me on the street and not assumed that I was stupid. Instead, they had looked at me as a person who probably knew how to read and could help them. And I did.

The boss

One day I went to work a little earlier than usual and arrived at the restaurant before Phương. A man was already sat at a table waiting for the reception to open. When I walked in I instinctively bowed my head to him and went to a room to change into my work clothes. When I returned I stood at the reception desk, next to the receptionist who was now at her workstation. The man got up to leave and I bowed my head to him again. I thought nothing of this, until I returned from my lunch break and Phương said that I had to go upstairs to meet somebody who had asked to meet me. I asked who this person was, as this was only the second time anybody had ever asked to see me. Phương said simply that I should go up to see the person. I was unsure, and a little scared, so asked Phương to please come up to the room to call on me if she hadn't seen me for a while. I was so nervous and was sweating as I walked up the stairs. I approached the room and knocked at the door. It was one of the karaoke rooms in the restaurant and the customer was on his own. It was the man I had seen in the morning.

Not knowing what to say I asked what he liked to drink. He said he would like a bowl of fruit and some mineral water. He asked what I would like to drink, but I declined. He asked politely if I would sit down, and asked how long I had been working at the restaurant. He also asked where I used to work, and I told him that I had worked with Phương previously and was working here now after a chance meeting with her. I had a strange feeling that he already knew my answers and maybe he was cross-checking my story.

There was a knock at the door, and I was relieved. It was Phương, who had brought the fruit and water. It was clear that she knew the man really well – and she looked at me with a smile. The man, whose name was Hung, asked Phương if it would be okay for me to stay there if I was not needed in the restaurant. Phương replied that it was fine, and called him 'boss'.

I was confused. What was he the boss of? We had lots of bosses frequenting the restaurant.

He turned on the karaoke machine and asked me to sing, but I declined. I said I couldn't sing. I sat there silently, and replied politely to his questions. To keep me occupied I started to peel a satsuma – and offered him half, as is customary in Việt Nam. The man asked if I liked to work at the restaurant, and he asked what time I started in the morning. After a while I asked to leave to use the bathroom, and when I left asked Phương who the man was. Phương said that he was the restaurant boss. I said that I had already met the boss, but Phương reassured me there were two bosses, and this was the second one. He had opened the restaurant with his friend. Now I was even more nervous, especially because he had asked lots of questions about my job. A short time after returning to the karaoke room I made my excuses and got up to leave, saying I had work to do.

For the next few days I had lots of questions swirling around my head. Why was the boss asking me so many questions? But I knew that I always worked hard, so had nothing to hide. He returned to the restaurant soon after and from that point on he was often there. I was always polite whenever I saw him.

On one occasion I had a phone call at the reception desk. It was Hưng and he invited me out to lunch. I said sorry, explaining that I was too busy with work. He must have been undeterred though because over the next weeks he called several times with the same request. Each time I declined. I thought that maybe he was just testing me to see if I would skip work to go out for lunch. I knew I had to be careful.

After a week or so Hưng asked me to the karaoke room again. This time I was even more nervous, and I needed a handkerchief to mop my brow. After an hour I asked to leave, and again returned downstairs to see Phương. She just smiled.

One day I finished work late, and as I pushed my motorbike outside I saw Hung. I bowed and said that I was working late because we had a large group. I started my bike and zoomed off. Some miles later, as I slowed down for a red light, I sensed that somebody was following me, although when I turned off the road there was nobody. The next day he invited me to the room again, where he asked me if I had a boyfriend. I said that I had had one once, but no longer, and he then asked if I'd far to travel to work. I told him where I lived previously, but again I felt that he already knew the information he was asking. In my head I now had some questions I wanted to ask him, although I knew that I couldn't. He was the boss after all. For a long time though I hadn't talked about my life and I was a little flattered that he showed an interest.

A week later Hưng again asked to meet him in the karaoke room. This time he told me that he had a friend who had a room to rent far closer to the restaurant than I was living, and asked if I would be interested. My heart was thumping like a school drum[26]. My hands were wet but there was nothing in the room to dry them on. I said that I couldn't possibly afford the room, but Hưng said that he would pay. I asked whereabouts the house was and when he explained I agreed to take a look. The house, down a narrow alleyway off Thợ Nhuộm Street, was

---

[26] In Việt Nam, schools use a large drum to signify the start and end of classes.

right in the centre of the city. It had three storeys and the ground floor was vacant. It would obviously be much more convenient to live there than in the small place on the outskirts of the city with my sister. Hưng said he only wanted to help me and, believing him, I agreed to move in.

A gift of jade

So I moved, with just a few of my belongings at first as I didn't know how it would go. I was nervous initially, and after the first night I actually returned to my home with Lien. Only slowly did I feel comfortable enough to make the move permanent. Hưng must have noticed my reluctance and started to have things introduced to my room – a TV, then a CD player, and then an electric fan. He asked for nothing in return.

Sometimes, we would meet up in the room at the restaurant to sing karaoke. I still declined his invitations to go out with him and he would occasionally ask why. I told him that I would only go out with somebody who loved me, never with somebody who only helped me. But the truth was I had grown really fond of him – although of course in Việt Nam it wasn't culturally acceptable to show any affection at this stage. Looking back, I believe it was the fact he showed any kind of affection towards me that made my heart yearn ever-so-slightly for him.

Although Hưng was persistent in his requests he was always very polite and didn't at any time push me or make me feel uncomfortable. I felt I could trust him. Of course, I knew that he knew a lot about me and I knew little about him. I felt that it wasn't my place to ask him. He was very amiable and charming and we laughed a lot. He was also very adept at deflecting any questions whenever I began to ask him. Eventually, I said that he was "khó hiểu" (difficult to understand). He laughed and replied "người khôn ăn nói nửa vời để cho người dại nửa mừng nửa lo" (wise people ask half-heartedly, leaving fools half happy and half worried). It was a lovely and open-ended reply – and hilarious because I didn't know who was the wise person and who the fool. I feared maybe I was the fool though as I was clearly sat next to a man wiser than myself.

After spending more time with Hưng I eventually agreed to go out to lunch with him. Hưng had said that his friend had a 'chả cá lá vọng' (speciality fish dish) restaurant. It was a dish I had never eaten before and it needed a bit of skill to eat it. Hưng said that the food was so tasty that a kiss following the meal would be bliss. He was joking of course, as the dish included the notorious 'mắm tôm' (fermented shrimp paste). I laughed and blushed at the same time at the mention of a kiss. I felt slightly exhilarated with this new world, and the person leading me there was very beguiling.

The next day Hưng asked me to go to the karaoke room with him. He handed me a beautiful jade bracelet and said simply that it was for me. I felt confused and didn't know what to say. At the same time Hưng held my arm and placed the bracelet on. It was a tight fit, but he had already prepared for this by rubbing something slippery on to it so that it didn't hurt. By now I was so red-faced that I thought I was going to suffer from heat stroke. Slowly, I was falling under his spell.

Phương must have noticed that Hưng and I were spending more time together, and the next time I asked to leave for a lunch date she didn't say anything to make me feel uncomfortable. Our dates would always be somewhere that I had never been before, eating dishes that were new to me. The dates were getting longer, although the time seemed to fly by.

Looking back on this time after so many years have passed, I realise that Hưng was the person who taught me to laugh. When we were together I smiled a lot, and for the first time in my life I felt truly relaxed around somebody.

After three months in my new flat I invited Hưng to see it. I knew he must have wondered how I was keeping it. With just the two of us there, and in the privacy of the flat, my feelings for him bubbled to the surface. I told him that I was suffocated by his charm. He put his arms around me and we embraced for the first time. I felt time fly by in his arms.

Later that day he asked me if I would like to go out to eat. I declined his invitation because although I was excited by our embrace I also felt embarrassed by our intimacy. In response, he simply kissed me lightly on my cheek and left. The room was calm and I slowly wound down from the earlier excitement. In any case, it was time for me to return to work at the restaurant, so I started to prepare for the afternoon shift.

As soon as I reached the restaurant I met Phương. I felt as though she could almost smell the scent of Hưng on my body, so I just kept quiet and busied myself with work. Eventually, Phương pulled me to one side and told me that Hưng was married and still lived with his wife. I felt myself blushing as I'd never blushed before. It was a choking wave of hurt that enveloped me – an instant, deep sadness that I couldn't control.

I was crushed. To be told this on the very day we had been so intimate made it all the worse.

The following day Hưng called the restaurant and asked to speak with me. He asked how I was but I answered only robotically. He clearly realised that something was not okay and the next day, when I arrived at the restaurant, he was already there at the door waiting for me. I bowed as usual and went to the changing room to prepare for the day. Hưng asked if I would go out for lunch with him, but I declined. Over the next few days he tried many times to engage me in conversation. But I avoided him. He must have sensed that my aura had changed – our intimacy was not as innocent as it had been the week previously.

A few days later I asked Phương if I could take three days off. I had tried to avoid Hưng's advances and I could tell that he knew something was wrong. I told Phương that I had been invited to the seaside resort Sầm Sơn by a friend's family. I knew the family from my time at the station – they used to look after the public toilets there. I knew that they liked me, and saw me as a model for their children to follow. The family had managed to get cheap rail tickets as the father was a train driver and said the whole trip would cost just 500,000 đồng each, for everything. Phương agreed, probably because she thought I had been asked away by Hưng.

I called Hưng and told him that I was going away for a few days with a good family and their three children. He said that was okay and agreed to hold my keys when I left (to the flat and my motorbike). I went to the tennis courts where he played each morning and asked him to return the keys when I got back to Hà Nội.

On the journey I confided with the eldest daughter, Hang – who was about my age – about what had happened. I told her that I was in love with a married man. I wanted to see how she reacted. Hang had been to school and I felt that I needed to see how somebody educated would respond. I felt in this way I could gauge how I should behave. But Hang asked only superficial things, like how he looked; was he handsome; was he romantic? She asked what he was like and I replied only that he had everything. Hang must have told her mother because later on she, Hang's mother, spoke with me and told me that it sounded as though Hưng had a lot of experience and would know how to handle the situation.

In any case, I had a lovely three days at the beach. It was only the second time I'd ever been to the seaside.

A Dream

When I returned to Hà Nội I went straight to my flat and Hưng was waiting. I asked if he'd been there long and he said not long at all. He handed me the keys to the flat and the motorbike. He also said that he had changed my motorbike to a new one as the old one was getting too old. It was a brand new Honda Dream. To own such a bike in 1997 was – literally – the dream of almost every Vietnamese. It was clear that he wanted to show in some way his affection for me. For whatever reason we were drawn together like magnets – the days we had spent apart had not weakened in any way my feelings towards him. Despite the complications I wanted this moment to last forever.

Later I asked Hưng about his family and he told me that his wife had the same name as me. Hưng had two daughters and they all lived together. He was ethnically Chinese. I asked how he had met his wife because it transpired she was just a few years older than me. Hưng, who was 38 at the time, replied that he met her while she was working at one of his businesses. In my head I thought that perhaps I would be the next woman to be his wife. Innocently, I asked how many wives a Chinese man could have. I was naive – and had no idea of different cultural traditions. He gave me a warm smile and said that if anybody wanted to marry him he would happily agree. I realised then how absurd my question had been.

Over the next few days I thought of little apart from the situation I now found myself in. I questioned myself constantly. Did I really want a life with Hưng under these circumstances? I wondered if I could look after him better than his wife did. Of course, I had no idea – after all I knew so little about her. Finally, I came to the conclusion that my situation was too complicated to sustain, mainly because I had mixed my personal and work life. To make matters worse, I knew that his home was very close to the restaurant. It was time to simplify things by separating my work and private life. So, I quit my job.

This time though I had left a job without having a replacement, and after a month of looking I still had no new work. Hưng had visited me several times over the month, and eventually suggested that I try another path and apply for a different type of work. I said that I had already been thinking along the same lines, but hadn't reached a final decision. I also told him that I was shy – and afraid that I might end up hurt. I told him that I didn't want his wife to know about me – and didn't want to be suffocated by his love for me.

First steps

I felt that I needed to choose an occupation that I could learn quickly – to give me the security I needed. I decided to train as a hairdresser's assistant and found a salon not too far from my flat. I paid about 1,200,000 million đồng to become a trainee, learning to wash and dry hair and help with other chores around the salon. During this time I met Hưng less often, although we would often speak on the phone. I had already told him that we had to be careful. I was also telling myself to be more cautious. I knew that Hưng had a family and didn't belong to me, and I knew that I had to keep my feelings for him to myself. But the reality was I missed him far more than I would have expected. He was experienced and knew how to care, and I felt safe when he was around. He always referred to me as 'em yêu', which although means 'my love' is more a friendly, warm way to address somebody. He would give me the magazines that he had finished reading, especially 'The Giới Đàn Ông' (Man's World). He didn't know that I couldn't yet read anything other than the few words I'd learnt from the streets.

The desire to read properly was growing all the time and I constantly looked for opportunities to learn. I would still ride around on my motorbike noting what shops sold and looking at their names – hoping to make the correct links. I was slowly improving though and could now at least read slowly – so long as the words were printed. I still couldn't read a handwritten letter, and couldn't yet write at all. But I knew that the next step must be to learn to write and so I bought a notebook and pen.

As Mao said: 'a journey of a thousand miles starts with the first step' – for my journey it was learning the alphabet, and my progress was painfully slow.

So many times my efforts ended with me bursting into tears. My writing was so ugly. In Việt Nam at the time, as is still the case, there is a great premium placed on neat handwriting and students are marked down for scruffy work. The result is that the average person writes extremely neatly. When I looked at my efforts in comparison to others' this seemed to highlight the mountain I had still to climb. It seemed to confirm my status in life – as somebody who was effectively an orphan, with nobody to turn to for help. No matter how hard I tried I just couldn't seem to make the letters look like they should. It was deeply frustrating and added to my sense of inferiority.

Of course there was nobody there to comfort me in these low moments. The only person I wanted to ask was my mother, or rather her spirit. I would ask her why she had ever given birth to me in the first place and left me to such a humiliating fate, with nobody and nothing there to protect me from this shame. I felt that I didn't even have a relative who I could turn to, particularly because those closest to me – like my sister Liên – were in a similarly difficult position to myself.

I seemed to be going around in circles, getting more and more frustrated with my situation and apparent inability to progress. But on one particularly distressing day, after shedding too many tears, I stood in front of a mirror to take a hard look at myself. Peering back was a girl with a swollen face, red nose and red eyes and I told myself that looking this way was simply making the already ugly world even uglier. I realised things had to change and I asked that person to stop crying. I told myself that a weak ego was no reason to cry, and that I wasn't to prejudge the future. I told myself that there was nobody to blame for my situation and I had to dig deep and carry on. I determined there and then that I would carry on, but this time in stoical silence. No more tears.

I also began to think that to speed up my progress with writing I needed to do something differently. I cast around, desperately looking for some outside influence to help me. I remembered, from my days spent at the train station, once hearing some people talking about the use of votive paper[27] to cast a spell on others. If this technique worked for other people, then why not for me? So I decided to cast a spell on myself. Or at least to have a go.

After burning a piece of paper that I'd written on with my ugly writing I crushed the burned paper and tipped it into a glass of water. Then, with eyes closed, I poured the lot into my mouth. All seemed to be going well until a small piece of paper that hadn't burnt properly got wedged in my throat. A coughing fit managed to dislodge it and I spat the errant piece into my hand. I burst out laughing at the ludicrousness of my situation. Who knows if my spell worked, but in any case I pushed on with my efforts to read and write.

Three months had gone by at the salon and I was running low on money. Remember, I was paying for the training I was receiving. There seemed to be no sign that I would be taken on

---

[27] Votive offerings, mostly from special paper, are normally made to the spirits of ancestors in an effort to improve their situations in the afterlife.

as an apprentice within the salon so I decided to look around for a paid job at another place. Eventually, I found a smart hairdresser's on Hòa Mã Street, in a nice part of the city. I told Hưng that I now had a job and could look after myself. I told him that we had to stop seeing each other and he replied that he would respect my wishes.

As soon as the words were out I knew that it had been the right decision, and felt stronger because of it. I asked Hưng to cut all contact with me – including phone calls. I said that if I was unable to cope with the situation then I would contact him directly, but added that if he really needed to see me then he could do so only at my new workplace. I knew that I didn't want to be overwhelmed and drowned by the love I still felt for Hưng. I needed to move on, however difficult this was going to be.

Moving on

So my new job started and each day that passed I seemed to feel better. I was growing stronger and didn't feel that I had to hide anything anymore. It was quite liberating. Freedom and independence! Or so I thought.

But after two weeks or so Hưng passed by the salon and pulled up on his motorbike. I went outside to say hello, and he asked how things were going and whether I would like to go out for dinner. Although I feared it might be a bad idea the fact was I missed him terribly. I accepted his invitation.

We went for dinner and our conversation was very light. It was typical of Hưng – he was charming but would always try and deflect any serious topic. As usual I was left with questions and no answers. In his company I always felt too inexperienced to penetrate his defences as he was so adept at changing the subject, or moving it in a direction he was happy with. As ever I was left with clammy hands and a feeling that I was dumb in the presence of somebody with so much more experience.

But this time there was a difference. During the meal I had at least reflected further on our relationship, and afterwards I told him firmly that he now had to assume his family responsibilities. After all he had a wife and two children. I told him again that we shouldn't see each other.

Time went by and in many respects I was happy – I was in control of my own destiny. But despite my efforts my love for Hưng was still there and occasionally I would give in to it and call him. After all, he had given me something so special – more through osmosis than by teaching: he had given me confidence and helped me to mature. He had also given me a sense of optimism. He did this simply by being there for me to observe, and witness how he conducted his life.

This had always been how I developed – not through instruction but simply by observing. It had helped me through my childhood, allowing me to negotiate the difficult and sometimes dangerous environments I had grown up in. And now it had been the same with Hưng. He was much older than me – by almost 20 years – and he was established and confident. There was a consistency about him that I admired. Hưng had been the first person to really respect me and seem to truly want to help me have a better future.

When I was together with Hưng I had always been concerned about how people would view me. I was in a vulnerable position because of the nature of our relationship and the fact that to a degree he was helping fund my life. This was still the case after I had told him that we could no longer see each other. So, I called Hưng and said that by living in the flat he had paid for left me vulnerable to being called a 'gái bao' (a kept women – a sugar baby). I told him that I no longer needed any help and said that from now on I wanted to pay my own rent. Hưng said that I was absolutely not such a person and told me not to take any heed of what people called me, adding that he truly wanted to help me in life. He said he knew how tough things had been and that he wanted to help me to avoid meeting people who would hurt me. He said that if I had a lover please let Hưng 'know his face' because he would be able to read his intentions. Hưng said that he had rented the flat for me because he cared about me and wanted a better life for me. I thanked him but insisted that I pay for the flat.

Now, finally, I felt fully in control of my life. My feelings for Hưng were still there, but I would limit my calls to once every two weeks or so, and after a couple of months of this I decided not to call at all. But one day, out of the blue, he called me. He asked how I was and, as is the Vietnamese custom, asked how I was eating. The truth was I was eating very little as I felt sick at the very thought of food, and was living largely off fruit. I didn't say what the cause was, but Hưng insisted that I went to visit a traditional medicine doctor.

My own previous visit to a doctor of any sort, other than the one occasion at the hospital, had been with Toàn when I was pregnant. This time, Hưng said that he knew the doctor very well and could vouch for him. He knew I was worried about going, but Hưng reassured me that all would be fine. He said I simply had to mention Hưng's name when I got to the address.

The doctor examined me – checking my eyes and looking at my skin. He said that I needed medicine to boost the effectiveness of my liver. The doctor gave me a month's supply of traditional medicine and each day I had a mixture to prepare. When I went to pay I learned that Hưng had already arranged to settle the bill. The next day Hưng came to the salon and gave me a small, slow-cooker with which he told me to cook the daily mixture of dried twigs, roots and herbs. This involved stewing the mixture and then drinking the juice once cooked. It was a lovely smell and the resultant juice was quite pleasant to drink, with a slight taste of liquorice.

A month passed and I called Hưng to thank him. I was feeling much better, although I still had no appetite and was losing weight. One day Hưng was passing the salon and waved at me. I went outside for a quick talk with him and when I returned my workmates quizzed me. They were older than me and each had, or had previously had, a husband. They guessed by watching us that we were in a relationship and I confirmed this when they asked me. I didn't elaborate too much on my situation though as we were always very busy and I thought that the others had their own lives to worry about.

Now all my effort was channelled into my work, and learning to read and write when I was at home. But progress, particularly with my writing, was still slow – painfully slow. Where I wanted straight lines of uniform letters to be I saw instead what looked to be the scrawlings of a worm that had slithered across the page. Every time I looked at my work I felt humiliated. It seemed that the mountain I was attempting to climb was still too steep. I was certainly too ashamed to write in front of anybody. If ever I was asked to write anything, such as filling in a form, I would ask a friend for their help. Internally, I would scream with frustration – made worse by my knowledge that it was the same for my siblings. None of them could, at that time, write. Our family had nothing to be proud of – and as each year passed our humiliation only grew.

Now, although we were no longer contacting each other, I felt as though Hưng was aware of what I was doing in my life. I would occasionally ride past the tennis court where he played each morning just to see him without him knowing. I always regretted doing this as it invariably made me feel worse.

One time a workmate at the salon, Nhung, said to me that a man such as Hưng would be a good lover but poor husband. I kept reminding myself of Hưng's wife and children in my efforts to move on from him.

Nhung and I were becoming close friends and would often go out together after work. She was married but separated and lived at home with her parents. Nhung was becoming like a big sister to me, and her family seemed to welcome me into their home. At one point we were hanging out with each other so much that one of the customers asked if we were in a relationship.

The salon, which was called Hương Rose, had a good reputation and the clients tended to be the well-to-do of Hà Nội. My wage was low but tips tended to be good, and the boss's mother would cook us lunch each day. The only issue was that any damage to equipment had to be paid for by the staff – and because the salon was high-class things tended to be expensive. Scissors, for example, cost up to $1,000, which in 1997 was an awful lot of money. This had the effect of making us extremely careful at work.

Generally, clients were served by whoever was next in line to work, but the best tips came from requests – when I was asked by somebody to serve them. I was mainly washing hair and head massaging, and helping the stylist with preparations. Huong, the owner, had a very good reputation as a top stylist and she had a lot of regular customers. The salon was extremely busy and the work surprisingly varied. Of course with tips being so important to us work days were long and hard when tips were scarce. Another of my workmates, Trang, once said during one of the rare quite times at the salon that to encourage customers to tip she felt like placing a sign around her neck saying 'Bọn em không sướng được bằng lông' (We can't afford to live on salaries alone). As often with Vietnamese humour, the funny twist was through a slight change in emphasis or tone producing a radically different meaning. In this case translated as 'We can't achieve orgasm from your hair alone'. In other words, please give us a tip.

By now I had been paying for my own rent for six months or so. I was truly independent and felt to some extent that I had regained my innocence. I would still occasionally speak with Hưng over the phone and he would often ask me to go for a drink, although I always declined his offer. I was simply focussed on my work and my efforts to educate myself. To reflect my new-found independence I changed my hairstyle and bought a few new outfits. This helped in boosting my confidence.

A Westerner calls

One day at work it was my turn to eat lunch – I was the last to eat as I'd been busy. But just as I was getting ready to leave the salon a Western man walked in. My first thought was, oh no another delay to my lunch – I'm going to be hungry now. But somehow, at the back of my mind, I had the most peculiar feeling. It was that I had to cherish this moment as this man may be my future husband. The feeling came from nowhere and I really couldn't account for it. His eyes never seemed to leave me though, and the thought at the back of my mind would not go away. By now two of my colleagues had returned from lunch, and it was my turn to go. As I left the salon I tried to rid my mind of this peculiar thought.

After my lunch I started to help Huong's mother with the cleaning up, but she told me to return to the salon. I said that I wouldn't be needed in the salon as there were three people working and only one customer. Besides, I still felt peculiar – embarrassed even – by my own thoughts. So I effectively hid in the kitchen.

When I eventually returned, the Westerner was having his hair washed by one of my colleagues. When this was finished he asked for a hot drink – so I was sent over the road to buy a hot Lipton's tea from the café opposite. When I returned I heard my colleagues asking him what he did and where he was from. He drank his tea and went to settle his bill. But when the bill came he commented at the high cost of the tea and hair wash, saying in Vietnamese that he preferred to pay Vietnamese prices not 'special' Westerners' prices. We all burst out laughing as the truth was he had been charged double.

However, despite this the Westerner returned the next day for another hair wash, and again ending with a cup of hot tea. But he didn't leave a tip, and my colleagues joked he was a 'Tây ky bo' (mean Westerner). He came back the next day, and the day after, and the day after that. In fact he soon became a regular fixture at the salon.

After a couple of weeks Huong asked if he would like a haircut, saying that he must be getting bored with just a hair wash each day. He agreed, but when Huong was mid-cut the unthinkable happened and she slipped with the trimmers and took a big chunk out of the top of his hair. Huong was silent, but it didn't get passed the customer, whose name was Steve. He laughed and told Huong that it really didn't matter as fortunately he was tall and nobody could see the top of his head. We all burst out laughing.

As time went on I noticed that the others struggled to understand Steve's accent and would often misunderstand what he was saying. Added to this was the fact that they enjoyed a laugh and would often be doing most of the talking, and rapidly at that. I began to notice that I was the only person in the salon who seemed to properly understand what he was saying – at least most of the time. I began to find myself 'translating' what he said to my colleagues – strangely, from Vietnamese to Vietnamese. At the same time Steve would often turn to me when somebody was speaking to him too quickly and ask for my help.

Why me?

As time went by my colleagues began to relax around Steve and become more and more friendly. One day one of the girls asked him why he kept coming to the salon. She said that it must be more than just for a hair wash. Steve agreed and said he mainly came to seem me, to which my workmate asked why me and not one of the others. Steve said that it was because I was the most beautiful woman in Hà Nội. Although I wasn't there at the time, I was of course mortified that he said this in front of my colleagues. I knew that at least two of them were looking for a partner so I was especially embarrassed to have had this attention directed at me. I told them that I had no idea he liked me, saying that we had never even had a proper conversation so had no clue. They explained that they now knew that he liked me a lot and the way they were questioning me seemed to suggest that they suspected I had met Steve outside of work hours. I replied that I was unaware of his intentions, and in any case I told them I knew that they were looking for partners not me. I said that I knew no English so couldn't speak to him properly. But they said that I wasn't to worry – they had asked everything about him so would fill me in.

From that point, whenever Steve turned up at the salon my colleagues seemed to do everything they could to make sure that it was me who served him and not one of them. Each day he would come and I would quickly wash his hair. Steve was easy to deal with – his hair was short and quick to wash and, besides, was already clean from the previous day. But even though I spent less time with him than any other customer he always returned and was always polite. The problem was his timing. I thought to myself, why does he always seem to come at my lunchtime – and why, every day, does he ask if I'm well? Is he not bored with the answer?

One day I was busy with another customer and somebody else had to wash Steve's hair. As I glanced over I saw that through soapy suds he had one eye open and was looked over at me – how that soap must have stung.

By now, even regular customers were asking why the Westerner was so often in the salon. Some of our customers worked regularly with foreigners and they said that he seemed to be easy going and an honest person. Some even said that they'd seen him elsewhere and he seemed to be on his own, in other words he had no partner. They said he seemed to be a nice guy. Everyone seemed to have the same thoughts when they met him. I went a lot on what they said as I had so little experience, and told them that he was learning Vietnamese and would come to the salon to practice.

One day Steve arrived at the salon while I wasn't there. He said he had come to give me a gift, and he left it with a workmate. When I returned to the salon my colleagues excitedly gave me the box and waited for me to open it. They were far more excited than I was. When I opened it my jaw dropped. It was a watch made out of plastic. I silently returned it to the box not knowing what to think. Steve seemed to have given me a cheap watch which I felt was in the style a younger person might like – and it certainly didn't seem to value me very highly. Later that day Steve arrived at the shop while I was having lunch. My workmate told him that I didn't like the present, and it seemed to be inappropriate, childish even. He looked shocked, but reassured my colleague that if I didn't like it he or I could return it to the shop and exchange it for one I liked. He said that the shop had only just opened in Hà Nội and was the trendiest watch-maker from the West at that time – Swatch. He left the shop address, and said he hoped I would find a more suitable timepiece.

After work I went to the Swatch store with Nhung, my closest workmate, and showed the watch to the receptionist. I asked if it would be possible to replace it. She was very kind and reassured me that there were a lot to choose from. I was shocked when I saw the high prices of these plastic watches. The next day I showed my colleagues my new watch and told them that they were not at all cheap. When Steve arrived the next day I felt slightly embarrassed for thinking that he was a cheapskate when I had first seen his present to me.

So now I had a new, purple, plastic watch. Still not to my taste and still very plastic – but at least it had not been intended to humiliate me, which is what I feared at first.

Trang, who was the bubbliest of all my workmates, once asked Steve if he could quantify his love for me. He thought for a moment and replied "anh thích em ấy hơn xe máy của tôi" (I like her more than my motorbike). Trang was horrified. "You can't say that!", she said. "You should say something like 'I love her more than my parents'" – something of that magnitude. "And what's worse", she said, "your motorbike is very cheap – not even worth that of Lan's". I knew Steve was joking and only pulling Trang's leg, although she didn't get the joke. Steve simply smiled and replied "yes, more than my mum and dad".

On one visit to the salon Steve asked me if I would like to go for a drink. I declined. I wondered what we would talk about if we did go out, given our language barrier and different backgrounds. Furthermore, at that time especially Vietnamese women such as myself going around with foreign men would leave them easy prey for malicious gossip.

Time went by and one day Steve asked all of us out for an evening, and we all agreed. Everyone was so happy when Steve insisted on paying the bill at the end of the night, agreeing that he seemed to be a gentleman. I felt a little more reassured after this that his intentions with me were genuine.

More weeks passed and Steve again asked if I would go out for a meal with him. I declined again, but said that I would go if Nhung could accompany us. Nhung agreed, but said that she would bring along her new boyfriend, who spoke very good English. Again Steve paid for the meal and, afterwards, Nhung's boyfriend said that we should all go to a nightclub, the Queen Bee. I presumed that this was Nhung's boyfriend's invitation, which in Vietnamese culture means that he would pay. But when the bill came at the end of the evening it was given to Steve and he asked me why he had to pay for this as well. I asked Nhung, who spoke with Bình, and they agreed to pay half and half. Steve seemed happy with this and he left for home at the end of the evening.

Every day Steve would be at the salon, always asking for the same treatment – a hair wash and a tea. One February day he said to me that the next day I wasn't to do anything or go anywhere as he had already made a reservation. I was a bit surprised at this and asked why. He said that the next day was

Valentine's Day, and explained that it was a special day for couples. I was shocked as this was the first time he had mentioned anything to do with being a couple. But I thought that I would give him a chance to say something to me in private, so the next day I asked Nhung for her advice. I said that Steve had booked a table at a nice restaurant, but I made sure to give her the address and said that if I called for help she would know where to go. I arrived exactly on time and Steve was already there.

The restaurant was in an old French-built villa in one of the nicer parts of the city. It was obviously a lovely restaurant and he took me upstairs to a table for two which had a red rose in a vase in the middle of the table. Steve helped me into my chair and was very polite. I had never been treated like that and it slightly put shivers down my spine. It seemed I was being treated like a princess, although I didn't know if this suited me or not.

The menu was entirely in English and Steve described the different dishes and asked me to choose. I was grateful that he was there to make me feel less absurd to be sitting in such grand surroundings looking at a menu in a different language. He spoke really quite good Vietnamese and in between the different dishes I was comfortable enough to ask him why he had said I had to accompany him today. He said that the 14th of February was a special day for couples who loved each other to go out. I had no knowledge of this day – and, once he'd said this, I had no real memory of the food I was eating or for that matter anything that was said from that point on.

In my head I was spinning – could it be that my caution around men because of what had happened was making me miss experiencing genuine affection? I was overwhelmed with thoughts and when I returned home that evening I started to run through my memories of this foreign man. I thought of all of his small kindnesses and actions. It seemed as though maybe he really did care for me.

The happy florist

By now everybody who came to the salon knew our story and all were in agreement that Steve and I should be a couple. One day a Malaysian customer gave me an enormous hardback English/Vietnamese dictionary, saying it was a gift to help me speak with him. I looked at this weighty book and thought it must be for somebody who was already highly educated, not for somebody such as me who was still fighting with the letters of the alphabet. Having never seen a dictionary before, I had no idea how to even search for a word.

It was the eve of the Tết celebrations and at the salon we were so busy. Everybody was receiving gifts from their regular customers and, of course, Steve arrived for his usual hair wash. When finished he asked Trang what Vietnamese women liked as Tết presents as he had no idea. Trang said that Vietnamese women liked flowers – those with petals made of paper money. He laughed and left, but returned later that day as we were preparing to leave, clutching a huge bunch of deep red roses in his arms. He'd ridden to the salon on his motorbike using just one arm, with the other wrapped around the flowers. But with his too-casual clothes and huge motorbike helmet that us girls used to call the slow-cooker he looked really quite ridiculous.

When he gave me the flowers the girls in the shop stopped to cheer and applaud. Steve wished us all happy Tết and held out the flowers for me. I took the flowers but wondered why there were so many in the bunch. I thought this man must be crazy. I told Steve that I would see him when the shop reopened after the Tết holiday. When I counted the roses there were 60, so I said to the girls I had no idea where to put them and gave them each a bunch to take home. They calculated that being the eve of Tết each flower must have cost at least 20,000 đồng – so we guessed the flower seller must have been very happy.

On my first day back at the salon I called at Steve's flat on the way to work. He lived in the same road as the salon and it was my first visit. I was clutching the dictionary as I had decided to give it to him. It was no use to me after all. I knocked at the door and it was clear Steve was still asleep. Eventually the door opened and I nervously pushed the dictionary into his hands and said that I had to go to the salon, before turning on my heels and walking briskly away. Later that morning he came for his hair wash and the first thing he said was "thank you for this morning". The horror. The girls looked at me with knowing glances – imagining that I held a secret that they were unaware of. When he had left for work they turned to me and asked if their eggs had been in the correct net, in other words were their suspicions correct.

The next day Hương asked Steve if he liked loving a Vietnamese woman. Was it different to a Western woman? I was mortified because I knew what they were thinking – and I'd only given him my dictionary. But my silence seemed only to incriminate me in the eyes of my workmates. Eventually I said that Steve was too honest and answered all of their questions without thinking. I said that the more he answered the happier they were and the happier they were the more questions they asked. The result was that my colleagues were now convinced we were a couple through and through.

Over the next few weeks I went out with Steve several times. Sometimes we would go for a drink, other times we would go to watch some musicians. I had never envisaged this new life but I tried to give him the opportunity to show me what his life was like. On one occasion he asked me if I would be his girlfriend, but I just looked at him with a gentle smile. He said that I didn't have to answer straight away but when I had made a decision to please let him know. We were always very polite with each other.

Weeks went by and each day Steve would come to the salon. But I still hadn't given him an answer, so was surprised when one day he asked if he could meet my parents. I asked why and he said that he knew that in Vietnamese culture a groom had to ask the permission of his potential bride's parents. He said that he wanted me to know that he was serious about me and wanted to reassure my parents about his intentions. I said that I understood, but was still scared about this new development. I was terrified of having to explain my family situation, and terrified of him learning that I wasn't a virgin.

A very beautiful place

Sometime later, one of my customers came to the salon. She knew about Steve and asked how serious we were. She said that men were men, whether they be Western or Vietnamese, and could be as faithful or otherwise. But the only thing she could say for certain was that whatever happened our children would be beautiful indeed.

By now I knew lots about Steve, much of it from customers – friends of friends who worked with him. My colleagues had asked him countless questions and I felt that I was beginning to know him well. Of course he still knew little of my situation. On one occasion he asked if he could visit me at my flat, but I didn't think this was appropriate and simply said that where I lived was near to his office. In truth it was little more than around the corner from his office, but I was very reluctant to let anybody know where I lived.

One weekend, Steve asked if I would like to go with him on a picnic. He said that he knew of a really beautiful location. I accepted his invitation and said that I would buy the food for the picnic – bread, pate, smoked ham and cucumbers, along with some cans of drink. This was the first time I ever rode pillion on his motorbike. It was a big step for me, as in Việt Nam at the time it would leave me vulnerable to nasty comments from passers-by. But I was happy to do this as we were travelling to the countryside – where nobody knew me. When I climbed on to his bike I felt like a monkey on the back of an elephant, such was our size difference. I couldn't see a thing.

In the end we travelled about 60km to the town of Hòa Bình, to the west of Hà Nội, and then started travelling uphill – the road winding through stunning limestone hills. After a while Steve said that the beautiful location was just ahead. I imagined something worthy of a scene from the side of a decorative vase. We bumped along a track through fields of paddy. Eventually we stopped – I presumed because the bumpy road was taking its toll on our legs. Steve said that we should rest and we parked the bike. I took out our picnic and we started to eat. I asked why we had stopped there and Steve said it wasn't just the beauty of the landscape but also the silence. I realised that this was his beautiful spot. I looked closer at the mounds of earth and small stone plinths and realised we were in the middle of a cemetery. Admittedly, it wasn't that easy to recognise it as such as the tombstones were small and simple. But it was a cemetery nonetheless. As if things couldn't have gotten more unusual Steve then repeated his question about me being his girlfriend. So there we were, surrounded by gravestones with me wondering how this man saw beauty in this scene. But I didn't feel scared, just puzzled at his choice.

I thought for a while and eventually said that I had some relatives in the area and asked if he would like to pay them a visit. I thought it was a good opportunity to slowly introduce some members of my family to him. I said that I couldn't yet give him an answer to his question because my family situation was very complicated and difficult. I said that once he had met my relatives I would ask him what he thought of them.

A night to remember

We set off, up a long winding road that snaked its way through the hills – past the houses of ethnic minority groups built on wooden stilts, and through lush forests. Eventually we arrived at a small town about 20km or so past Hòa Bình and went straight to the house of my aunt. She was delighted to see me, although clearly shocked that I had arrived with a Western man. I explained my situation, telling them that Steve and I had been picnicking and he had asked to meet my family.

From my aunt's house we walked down a lane towards my elder brother Long's place. He had eventually moved out of our father's house and bought a small piece of rocky land with a simple hut to live in, not far from our aunt's house. It was very cheap land and my brother was trying his hardest to make a go of it as a small farmer. He had put in a lot of effort in his attempts to prepare the land – ready to plant sugarcane, which was the popular crop in the area. We briefly said hello to Long and exchanged a few words, and then returned to my aunt's house.

By now other members of the family had arrived and all were really surprised at their guests. They insisted that Steve and I stay for dinner, despite me saying that we were only paying a quick visit. The questions were coming in thick and fast and excitement was spreading. More family members arrived – clearly intrigued at their unexpected guests. Eventually there were too many people to sit for dinner and guests had to be split into two groups. They sat me next to Steve, mainly so that I could translate for them.

When they found out that Steve could speak some Vietnamese, the questions were rapid-fire. Of course the rice wine was flowing and everybody wanted to toast their guest. Eventually Long lent over and whispered in my ear that Steve shouldn't drink with the relatives because he had to ride the motorbike. I turned to Steve and told him what Long had said. But the relatives heard and the next thing they were insisting that we stayed overnight. Their welcome was incredible, as was their hospitality. Eventually, at around 9pm, everybody was looking for a place to sleep. I was ushered into a bed with the girls and my aunt, and Steve was taken to sleep in my uncle's bed.

In the morning, at around 6.30am, I went to the well with my aunt to collect water, and then collected some hay to burn to warm the water for tea and for the men to wash their faces. Steve asked how I had slept and I replied "ngon" (fine). But I burst out laughing when I asked him and he said it was the first time in his life he had shared a bed with another man. He said that my uncle had slept like a log and snored throughout the night. Steve had had to keep still all night so that he didn't wake my uncle.

He asked to be pointed in the direction of the toilet and after a few minutes he returned and asked if he should sit down or stand up. I said for a number one stand and number two squat. He asked: both in the same place? I was a bit worried as the toilet was extremely basic – two small pieces of wood stretched across an open pit – and feared he might fall in, especially because he weighed a lot more than the average Vietnamese and the wooden struts were old. The 'door' was the cloth from an old sack. I had an idea – and told Steve that the best place to go would be behind some banana trees in the garden. I returned to the house and told my relatives to look the other way while Steve did his business.

After a cup of hot tea, I told my relatives that we had to return to Hà Nội as we each had to go to work. So we said our goodbyes and began our journey home. On the way I asked Steve what he thought of my relatives, especially my brother. He said that everybody seemed to be happy and good people and he had especially liked my brother. I was so relieved and touched that he felt this way about Long, who means so much to me. It was clear that Steve was an easy person to get on with as he seemed to take meeting my relatives in his stride. He clearly wasn't the kind of person who would look for difficulties. I started to relax, and tell him things about myself. I told him why I was living in Hà Nội, and that I had many relatives who were from the countryside. I said that if this didn't bother him then I would indeed be his girlfriend. I also said that I had already had a boyfriend. Steve simply held my hand and said that everything I had said only made him want to marry me even more. He said that we could often meet my relatives.

Decisions, decisions

Over the next days and weeks I started thinking a lot about my future. This was the first time anybody had wanted to marry me. I thought that Steve was kind, helpful and had a good job. He treated me really well and I started to think that I really did want to marry him. I began to imagine what my future might be, but was still worried about my personal circumstances. I turned to those closest to me who had more experience and asked for their advice. They all reassured me that Steve was genuine and different to most other men. It was now seven months or so since Steve had first walked into the salon.

One day on the way to work I called in at Steve's flat to show him some photos I had had taken. He commented on how beautiful they were and asked if he could possibly keep one to send to his family. I asked what he would say to his family and he said that he would tell them this was the picture of his future wife. My heart was once again pounding like a school drum.

This seemed to be true love now and my fondness for him was growing, although of course I was still reluctant to show it. That evening we were planning to go to dinner but we started talking and in the end realised we had forgotten to eat. Eventually Steve said that he had a couple of mangoes that we could eat. But when I watched how he prepared them I couldn't bear it. As he peeled each fruit he squeezed it and the juice ran down his arm. It was appalling and I didn't eat at all.

A few days later I took Steve to meet my old friend Phương, who had been the manager at the restaurant where I met Hưng. I knew that she had a lot of life experience so I valued her opinion. Sometime earlier I had introduced her to my aunt and uncle, who ran a travel business, and they were helping her get a passport and visa for Russia, where her husband had lived for the last over 10 years.

At the time I had said to Phương that if, after she arrived in Russia, she found a good job or even a good man for me then to let me know and I would follow her a month later. She was heading to Moscow to work with her husband. I had even given Phương a small picture of me to take with her.

Phương quizzed me about what our intentions were, and what Steve's family situation was. Later on she said that Steve seemed okay – at least he was certainly handsome. I guessed that she was probably concerned over his intentions towards me, so I reassured her that we were getting to know each other before becoming lovers

One late afternoon Steve said that he would like me to meet one of his friends, a man called Chung. Steve and Chung had worked together as teachers of English when he first arrived in Việt Nam in 1995 and the two were close. Steve asked me to go to a bia hơi (fresh beer) place near to the school where they used to work. When I arrived it was a typical bar scene – predominantly men sitting around drinking beer at plastic tables on the pavement. I walked over to their table and Steve introduced me to his friend. I could feel hundreds of pairs of eyes looking at me and I felt my confidence draining away.

I sat down feeling so self-conscious I didn't even order a drink. I wanted to be anywhere but this place. In typically Vietnamese style Chung straight away started to ask questions about my life and my family. It felt like an interrogation and I felt uncomfortable, but I gave him some basic information. Chung pushed me to tell him more, and his questions were clearly designed to find out if I was a 'good girl' or not. I was getting ready to leave when Chung asked me if I had been to school.

The question hit me like an arrow – it was the very question I always dreaded being asked and the one I always tried to avoid answering. Tears flooded my eyes and started to roll down my cheeks, and all I could do was gently shake my head from side to side. There was silence for a few moments and Steve had a panicked look in his eyes – clearly alarmed at what Chung had said. I said that I had to go and I quickly left the two of them.

When I walked to my motorbike the hundreds of pairs of eyes were looking at me once again. My make-up was running and I was aware that I was wearing clothes that were fashionable – possibly too fashionable in the present context. I could imagine what those eyes were thinking. I fumbled for my key but I felt clumsy and conspicuous. Normally my tears were reserved for private moments not for contexts such as these. I gritted my teeth and jumped on to my motorbike and rode off – all the time trying to avoid the hostile gazes. I felt humiliated and the harder I tried to hold in my tears the more I cried. I headed for my flat.

By the time I arrived home I felt as though every humiliation in my life had returned to grip hold of me. Hundreds of questions rattled around my head. I searched for answers, but none appeared.

The next day Steve came to the shop and straight away apologised for his friend. He said that he had no idea Chung was going to ask me such questions. But he also reassured me that his friend liked me. He said that I had come across as being an intelligent person. I gave Steve a gentle smile and told him that I was okay.

To Russia, with love?

I spent the next two weeks deciding that something really had to change in my life. I had two choices: marry Steve or follow my friend Phương to Moscow, where she would help me to get a job. I decided to go to Russia and I told Steve of my decision. He was clearly shocked and said he knew nothing of my plan. He asked why I was going. He then thought for a while before turning to me and saying that if I was determined and really wanted to go then he could come with me.

Over the next few days things returned to what had been normal. But I was questioning my decision to go to Russia and decided it was best to give things a little more time so that I could be more certain. I went out with Steve along with my friend Nhung. Steve was always happy if I brought a friend along because he knew that it was uncomfortable for me to be seen with a Western man on my own. I would ride my motorbike with Nhung riding pillion, with both of us following Steve. On one such evening I told Nhung of my friend's move to Russia, and said that I was planning to go myself. But she said that life there was little better than in Việt Nam, and she said I shouldn't go. I turned to Nhung and asked her why I seemed to have all of the opportunities that she wanted when I wasn't even looking for them. She was divorced and, with her son, had had to move back in with her parents. Nhung said that if it was my turn to wave the flag then I had to do it. We rode along in the flow of traffic as we headed to the bar.

Some days later I took Steve to visit some other members of my family. This time it was to visit my grandmother and uncle in their village home. Steve said that he really enjoyed the beautiful setting of their house, which was sat in a smallholding of fruit trees. He said that he was proud to know my family. Both my uncle and grandmother said they were happy that I had brought a friend to visit. My uncle had worked in Eastern Germany for several years and was particularly excited to speak German to Steve. I think he saw it as an opportunity to show off his language skills. The problem was Steve didn't speak German, other than a handful of words and a questionable song about a hat with three corners.

Steve clearly enjoyed the food that my family prepared. In fact it was one of the best things about visiting them – the food was always wholesome and delicious, usually involving one of their best chickens. After dinner my uncle continued to fire questions at Steve while I was helping with the washing up. I was flitting between the outdoor kitchen and the room where we'd eaten, and each time I returned I would hear only my uncle or grandmother talking, with Steve answering "dạ vâng ạ" (a very polite 'yes, indeed'), with the occasional "tôi hiểu" (I understand). It made me chuckle because it was all Steve seemed to be saying.

Once I'd finished tidying I took Steve to the back garden to walk through the fruit trees. I pointed out the different types: jackfruit, guava, longan and plum to name just a few. He said that he loved things that were simple and natural and was really enjoying himself. I felt as though I was a tour guide of the garden and felt I was doing a good job as I knew all of the trees. I also felt as though we understood each other without necessarily having to say a lot. We were always laughing, especially when Steve mispronounced a word. I wanted him to slowly get to know my family, a task made easier by the fact that he seemed genuinely excited at the prospect of meeting them. On occasions such as this he made me feel very comfortable and was clearly not judging me. There seemed to be no need for me to feel the humiliations that had plagued me for so many years.

Steve worked as a journalist and his hours were normally from around 2pm to 10pm or later, with mine 7.30am to 7.30pm. It meant that other than a Sunday the only times we could meet were at the salon. But occasionally we could get away from the city for a few hours and we would sometimes ride into the countryside surrounding the city. In those days you didn't have to travel far as the city was still fairly contained. I noticed the ease with which Steve would converse with children in villages or along roadsides. He used these trips as an opportunity to practise Vietnamese and would always make the children laugh. Ordinarily, children in such rural areas would be very shy, but Steve made them feel at ease and they clearly loved the fact that they had spoken with a 'Tây' (Westerner).

Sometimes, when we weren't busy, Steve would stay longer at the shop. He would stay for a second cup of tea, which made my boss's mum very happy as by now she was selling the drink.

On one occasion a beggar with missing legs appeared on the street outside of the salon. He had made a simple trolley out of a skateboard and was pulling himself along calling on passers-by to give him money. He was covered in bandages, some of which were soaked red. I knew the man and knew that to an extent at least it was a 'show', with the blood being fake. Steve looked at me and said that his father did the same in the UK – the only difference being that his father would drive himself by car to a different town to beg for money, and nobody knew why because he didn't need the cash. I was shocked but my workmates said that perhaps he was raising money for poor people.

Secretly I thought that it meant that his family may have a story as mine had. Perhaps it was difficult for him, and that's why he had had to come to Việt Nam to find a job. It seemed as though Steve may not be the perfect person I thought he was and I felt sorry for him that he may also have had struggles. Perhaps this was why he was so friendly when he met poor people, and never seemed to look 'down' on them. Maybe this was the background he was used to. I wasn't in the habit of asking about people's lives if they hadn't volunteered the information, but in Steve's case I was interested.

A diplomatic mission

One weekend I asked my uncle and aunt who lived in Hà Nội if I could bring along an English friend to meet them. I said that he wanted to speak to a member of my family. My uncle and aunt agreed and we arranged a time to visit – one evening after my work had finished. My relatives were a little surprised as it was the first that they had learned of my friend. They were even more shocked when, after our tea and biscuits had finished, Steve turned to them and said how glad he was to meet them and how grateful he was – and then said he wanted to ask for my hand in marriage. Since I hadn't mentioned anything to my aunt and uncle about my relationship with Steve, they were a bit shocked. My cousin, who could speak very good English, was also present and he turned to Steve and started speaking with him. I had no idea what was being said, I merely looked on and wondered. I heard my aunt and uncle saying that we would work together to bring two countries closer. I thought this was a tall task, but clearly – judging by Steve's expression – the conversation was going well. He seemed delighted that my family seemed to be giving him their support.

Later on, as we rode home, Steve told me that he had really enjoyed the evening. He always seemed to be polite and kind and I remember thinking that he had finally won me over. He made me feel confident about myself.

A few days later I asked Nhung to come with me to visit a fortune teller. We went to two different fortune tellers and each gave me a completely different outcome. I don't usually believe in such things – mainly because they always seem to tell people what they wanted to hear. It was really a bit of fun. I told Steve that one of them had said that we could marry this year and he was delighted. He asked if this were true. Was I sure I wasn't joking – telling me that it wasn't okay to joke about such things. I smiled and nodded that I wasn't joking.

The next day I went to the salon and broke the news. Everybody was so happy – and immediately started talking about our 'ăn hỏi' (engagement party). Things moved very quickly. I was given the option of five, seven, nine or more bridesmaids and ceremonial offerings – so long as it was an odd number. I chose seven – as it was neither too big nor too small, and also it had been my mother's name. Next I was asked about the colour of the 'áo dài' (traditional dresses). Huong did all the arranging for the engagement party. I had to think about where to bring this splendid entourage as normally it would be to the house of my parents. Nhung said that if I had nowhere to go her parents would surely offer their house as a venue. She said that her parents liked me a lot and would be very happy to help. This was so kind of her to offer, but in the end my uncle and aunt said that I could use their house and they would be the ceremonial hosts on behalf of my family.

In Việt Nam this was an exceptionally kind gesture. Traditional belief has it that in a house with unmarried children of similar age, such an act could bring about some form of bad luck – and at the very least it would be deemed a bad idea as such an act should be reserved for their children only.

So on the day of my engagement party my uncle and aunt would represent me. That left Steve. What to do about him, as he also needed representation? Again my friends stepped in and it was agreed that Nhung's father would represent Steve as a surrogate father, and Huong's mother would be his surrogate mother. Kind acts by each. The ceremonial gifts, including roast suckling pig, fruit, cake and money etc. were carried on red-lacquered ornamental trays by seven of my friends, each wearing pink áo dài and travelling on decorated cyclos, all the way from Steve's flat to my uncle's and aunt's house – a journey of several miles.

It was a beautiful, sunny day and things went as smoothly as they possibly could. This was in no small part because of the kind cooperation of family and friends. I am still to this day grateful for their kindness.

A place in the country

Now we were engaged, Steve said that he'd rented a house – a proper house with a garden rather than a tiny city-centre flat like the one he lived in when we met. He seemed very pleased with this new place – and told me that there was a small garden with grapefruit and starfruit trees. But best of all there was a pond on the neighbouring piece of land full of vegetation – especially morning glory and banana trees – and 'something special'. He said it was especially good because it was a bit like living in a city and a village at one and the same time. The house was nice enough – two bedrooms and a living room with a separate kitchen and a bathroom. Steve said 'something special' was yet to come – and I would find out what as dusk started to settle. I was intrigued, but burst out laughing when I heard this 'special' noise. It turned out that our neighbours were frogs – and lots of them too. I said that I thought I'd escaped this noise when I left the village all those years ago. Every night there had been punctuated with the sound of croaking frogs and toads. And now Steve had brought it back with a vengeance. To complete the picture there were also fireflies of a night time. The strange thing was, as time went on, after having been scared of such sights and sounds during my childhood, I began to find this noise and spectacle reassuring.

The house was down a small alleyway in Khâm Thiên district, an area well known for its government housing. There were lots of blocks of workers' flats, built for people who had worked in state jobs for many years, and all with 'add-ons' – makeshift extensions that flat-owners built to give themselves a bit more room.

And so we'd moved in together and started a new chapter in our lives. I gave up my job at the salon and we started planning for our wedding day. Steve told me that his father, Tony, and Aunt, Berna, would be coming over for the ceremony. He said that his father was terrified of flying and had never flown before, so his sister had agreed to accompany him.

Unexpected tears

We decided that our wedding would be in a city-centre hotel called the Hòa Bình (Peace), the name of the area Steve had taken me to for our first picnic. We had 120 guests, including my family and friends and many of Steve's colleagues from the newspaper. As is customary at wedding celebrations we went as a couple from table to table to greet our guests as they ate. Once we'd completed our lap it was time for the speeches. My father kept it simple – thanking the guests and wishing us happiness for the future – and Steve's father, using Steve's friend Chung as translator, gave his speech. But I wasn't expecting what he said. Steve's father said that he was honoured to be at the wedding on his son's special day, and said that there was one thing in particular that Steve and I shared and that was the fact that our mothers had died long ago and couldn't be with us to share our day. But he wished that their spirits would be looking down now and witnessing our wedding and hoped they would be proud and happy. I was so shocked hearing Steve's father mention my mother that I couldn't control my tears.

After our wedding Steve's aunt and father stayed in Hà Nội for a few days. Sometimes it would be me who showed them around because Steve would have to work. Mostly we went by taxi, although on one occasion I took Tony on the back of my motorbike for a tour around the city. Of course I still couldn't speak any English so I simply gesticulated to Tony to jump on the back. He was so nervous and he didn't take my advice and put his arms around me – preferring instead to grip the base of the seat. I tried to ride as smoothly as possible, and we went up to Hoàn Kiếm, where I dropped him at a café for coffee. I somehow managed to get across that I would return in an hour's time to pick him up, but when I returned the poor man said he'd prefer to go home by taxi.

Grey skies and instant noodles

A month or so after my father-in-law and Aunt Berna had returned to the UK, Steve and I travelled there to visit the rest of his family. The newspaper had given Steve a month's leave and I was as excited as I was scared by the prospect. I knew nothing of the West, other than what I'd heard about America. Of the UK I knew virtually nothing — only that Steve was looking forward to seeing his sister, who he was especially close to. I hoped that we would get along when we met.

But when we arrived I was in for a shock. It was wet, and the skies were grey. It was the middle of winter and we drove from the airport to Aunt Berna's house, where we were staying. Aunt Berna lived alone and Steve said that her house was very traditional. There were thick net curtains on every window, and the rooms were filled with old furniture. After a few hours Steve asked why I was spending so much time peering through the curtains, and I replied that I was wondering where all the people were. Of course in Việt Nam, life is lived outside and the streets, especially in the cities, teem with life. Here, in something Steve called 'suburbia', there seemed to be nobody. Just empty-looking houses with net curtains in every window.

Steve explained that in the UK most people travelled by car rather than motorbike. His Aunt had kindly lent us her car for a few days so that we could travel around and visit people and places. But this typically kind act was my undoing. The trouble was I wasn't yet used to travelling by car, and I was terribly travel sick. It was so bad that I was queasy for most of the four weeks – to the point that I couldn't really enjoy things.

Fortunately, I'd travelled with a box of instant noodles – 28 packets in fact. I think I had a packet a day as I also struggled with the dietary change to Western food. Steve's aunt wouldn't let me do anything in the house as we were her guests. She even insisted on washing my clothes. Can you imagine how strange that felt for somebody with my background? The trouble is she also wouldn't hear of me cooking, and I had to force myself to eat the very traditional English meals she would kindly prepare, which I found to be very bland. I felt so awkward because my car sickness was making my fear of mealtimes even worse, and I didn't want to spoil Steve's visit home to see his family.

Other than meeting my in-laws, the one highlight of our trip was a few days spent in an old water mill in the Welsh mountains. The beautiful old mill was on the slopes of a hill next to a raging river, apparently swollen by all the rain that had fallen prior to our visit. The cascading water roared as it passed beside the mill and the whole scene was like a painting. I couldn't believe where we were – and felt like a princess who'd awoken in a dream-like setting.

Bà Nga comes to stay

Back in Việt Nam I swiftly recovered and within a few months I was pregnant with our daughter. We decided to invite my grandmother, Bà Nga (Grandmother 'Russia'), to stay. Although she was by now in her late 80s, she was very fit and active. But I knew that her life in the village was difficult – she was always working, doing chores around the house, such as picking vegetables or preparing food for the pigs. It was hard manual work, especially preparing the pigs' food. One of the things they ate was the bark from banana trees. It was Bà Nga's job to sit astride a felled tree and shave off the bark using a large, sharp knife. My uncle had quite a few pigs to feed so this task in particular was very strenuous. Each time I visited her I would always tell her she needed to start taking it easy.

Sitting there chewing her usual concoction (areca nut, betle leaf and lime) she would glance up at me with mild contempt, and say with a huff: "gớm chết. Không làm thì ai làm cho?" (if I don't do it who will?) The fact was, although the house belonged to her she was well aware that in rural Việt Nam at the time unless she had a role in the household her standing within it would be greatly diminished. I would tell her to let uncle, aunt and their children do the work but she would reply: "con ơi. Nhà có một trăm nghìn việc. Ai cũng có việc làm" (there are thousands of things to do in a house. Everyone must have work to do). I told her that I liked to see her relaxing and chewing her mixture, which as well as giving her a mild buzz also made her teeth jet black. In the olden days it was thought that white teeth were the sign of an uncultured person.

On one visit, Bà Nga asked me to help her prepare the mixture, which involved crushing and mixing a betel leaf, areca nut and the lime in a small brass pot. She laughed, saying that she had only a few teeth left so needed all the help she could get. It took about ten minutes of constant mixing, after which Bà Nga scooped out the mixture and popped it into her mouth. Intrigued, I asked if I could try a mixture as I had no idea what it was like. She handed me some and we both sat there chewing away. I noticed that she always had streaks of red down her lower lip whenever she took the mixture.

I started to feel a tingling sensation inside my mouth and feel a bit light headed. I asked Bà Nga if this was normal. She replied that it had no effect on her. Bà Nga looked at me and started to stroke my leg affectionately. I said that the next time we came to visit her we would take her back with us to Hà Nội for a few months. Politely, she agreed, although I don't think she thought I was at all serious. I, on the other hand, was delighted that she had agreed at all.

I told my uncle and aunt that I planned to take Bà Nga to Hà Nội for a few months. They agreed, so long as Bà Nga did the same, and the very next week we hired a car to drive to the village to collect her. In Hà Nội, Bà Nga seemed to settle in quickly into her new life, which was spent entirely in the house and garden, although she went a bit quiet when I said that she would stay with us for six months. She had company in the house, because I had also invited my cousin Huyền, one of Bà Nga's other granddaughters, to stay with us in Hà Nội to help with things and make sure her grandmother was comfortable.

It was six weeks into her stay with us until she agreed to our offer of taking her out for a trip around Hà Nội to see some of the sights. I said we were taking her to Hồ Chí Minh Square, where I knew there would be lots of people. Bà Nga rode pillion with me while Steve rode by himself. If it wasn't the first time she had been on a motorbike it was certainly the first for many, many years and Steve had to give her a bunk up on to the passenger seat. He told Bà Nga to hold tight. I started the engine and we were off.

As we rode along I told Bà Nga what to expect: the immaculate soldiers, the drama of the changing of the guard, the beautiful surroundings. I pointed out different things of interest as we rode, but to everything she said only "uh" (oh!). Eventually I asked if she was seeing the same things I was and she replied that she wasn't. I asked why not and she replied that her eyes were firmly shut – out of sheer terror. She said there was just too much traffic, with bikes and cars seemingly coming at her from all angles. She likened the traffic to 'lá tre' (bamboo leaves) in the village, blowing this way and that, and said the whole experience was making her dizzy. I said that when we got to the square we would rest a while and then head straight back home. It was a pity as just a few hundred metres down the road was the beautiful West Lake – a sight she would surely have enjoyed.

One day, Steve asked Bà Nga when the last time was that she had visited Hà Nội. She replied that she had only been to the city once and that was when she was very young – in her teens or early twenties. Steve was surprised as her village was so close to the city – only about 60km away. Bà Nga explained that she had been a wet nurse for a wealthy business family of Chinese descent, who had a house near Hoàn Kiếm Lake – in the very centre of the city. She said that the job was a fine one: not only did it give her money to send home, but it also meant she was given the best food the family had to offer. This was so that her milk would be full of nutrients for their baby. In particular she could remember eating monkey meat. When quizzed by Steve as to what the biggest differences were between now and then, she thought for a while before replying "ma túy" (opium), the acrid smell of which, from the numerous dens, drifted through the streets in whole areas of the city. But she had no idea of where exactly the house was. Like almost all rural women at the time she could neither read nor write.

One day Bà Nga said that she would return to the village the next day. I feared that we had upset her in some way and asked what we had done. I reassured her that this was her home and we wanted her to stay. But Bà Nga said that she worried how her son and his family were coping without her. I felt a twinge because my uncle was the last remaining of her nine children still alive. Several had died during the US bombing campaign and others had died from various accidents soon after. By the time I was born there were just three children left – two boys and a girl. But the girl was my mother and she died around 1980. That left just two and, tragically, my second remaining uncle – the elder brother – lost his mind from an infection following some dental treatment.

I had met him once many years previously and I remember he was kept in a locked room at his home – looked after by his wife and children. I was only allowed to speak with him through a small gap in the door, and I asked him if he knew who my mother was. He replied that she was in heaven. I knew that living with us had reignited some of Bà Nga's memories. I reminded her of the daughter she had lost – a fact she would often allude to whenever we had met previously.

In Việt Nam there are various subtle social cues, especially when you are a guest in somebody's house, and when I reflected on what Bà Nga had said I came to the conclusion that she was really just testing her welcome. In any case she didn't repeat the suggestion and soon days and weeks started to fly by.

There were certain idiosyncrasies with Bà Nga in our day-to-day living. We had two televisions at home, and Bà Nga insisted that the one Steve and I watched had the best programmes. This left Bà Nga with the second television, and in particular she enjoyed boxing whenever that was on. To watch her you would have thought there were three boxers in the ring – Bà Nga being the surprise addition. She would move, duck and weave as best she could when the punches came in. Whenever a punch was landed she would exclaim: "ơi trời ơi, chết con người ta rồi!" (oh my god, we're dead!). Bà Nga would speak over the top of any programme with a stream of unfiltered thoughts – especially when we were watching the news. As we often had CNN on the TV – short of anything else to watch – Bà Nga would always comment on the terrible state of the Western world with all of its fighting. On one occasion we heard Bà Nga roar with laughter and went into her room to see what was going on. On the TV the Spice Girls were going through one of their routines.

Bà Nga turned to us as we walked in and said they were celebrating because somebody had actually won a battle.

One day Steve asked what was happening to his book. He would always leave one on top of the toilet cistern so that he could have something to read while sat on the loo. He said that he couldn't understand why his book kept getting thinner every time he went to the bathroom. I laughed, realising that Bà Nga must have assumed it was there to use as toilet paper.

Occasionally, Bà Nga would ask for some pain relief. If mild, I would give her some ginseng, but if the pain was worse I would give her a paracetamol and codeine tablet, dissolved in a glass of water. One evening she asked for one of the tablets, after complaining of a headache, but said that she would take it in her own time so to just leave it on her table along with a glass of water. I did as she requested, but then a few minutes later when I went to check on her I saw her stood in the middle of the room with eyes like a startled rabbit – froth oozing from the corners of her mouth. She must have forgotten that the effervescent tablet needed to be in water for a minute to allow the fizz to settle, and instead popped the whole thing into her mouth. I could only imagine what she was thinking.

After about three months in Hà Nội Bà Nga said that it was finally time for her to return home. She said that it didn't matter how much we welcomed her she knew in her heart that it was time to go. I asked if there was anything she would like to buy to take back with her to give as a gift and she replied "một trăm cái bánh mì" (100 loaves of bread). I laughed and asked why bread. She replied that it would be useful and not cost too much. So the next day we bought two whole sacks of loaves and hired a car to drive to the village. Word would soon spread in the village that Bà Nga had returned and I knew the bread would be handed out as gifts to her many visitors. Young or old, all would get a loaf.

On our next visit I said how much we missed her and the time we spent together. As we rode off the words of an old nursery rhyme rattled round my head: 'bà ơi bà. Cháu yêu bà lắm. Tóc bà trắng, mầu trắng như mây. Khi cháu yêu bà cháu lắm bàn tay. Khi cháu vang lời, cháu biết bà vui'. (Gran oh gran, I love you so. Your hair is white – as white as a cloud. When I love you I want to hold your hand. When I obey you I know you are happy).

Bà Nga lived for another 16 years, and never again left her house. When she died the local government provided a band for her funeral as she was the most venerable woman of the village: at that point being the oldest ever resident at 105 years of age.

The buffalo

At around this time I had a worrying phone call from my relatives in Hòa Bình, whom I had introduced Steve to on our first trip together. My cousin told me that my brother had been arrested and was being held at the local police station. Apparently, he had been charged with killing a buffalo, which had been electrocuted by a fence Long had erected in an effort to protect his crop of sugarcane.

I knew from Long that he had been having trouble with buffaloes on his land and they had destroyed much of his first ever sugarcane crop. Long's farm was relatively isolated, and there were many buffaloes in the area. They roamed around freely, with each having a bell around its neck so that it could be heard by its owner.

I felt a chill as the story unfolded, and knew that Long was in big trouble. Buffaloes were valuable beasts, and were heavily used by farmers for many tasks. I knew that it would take a lot of money to have my brother released. Reparations would certainly have to be made to the owner of the buffalo, and there was sure to be a fine to pay.

It transpired that Long had panicked when he found the electrocuted buffalo, so quickly removed his electric fence. He had asked a local man he knew to help dispose of the other evidence – the dead buffalo – and together they had somehow heaved the beast on to a strong wooden barrow, which they pushed as far as they could manage away from the farm before dumping it.

But although they had successfully disposed of the carcass, it was found later that evening by the animal's owner. The police said that the buffalo's owner had simply retraced the wheel marks the heavily-laden barrow had made in the ground all the way back to Long's farm. It was an open and shut case. Long had been locked up straight away.

I told Steve that I would have to go alone, because any sight of a foreigner would only increase the amount of money I would have to pay for Long's release.

Long had been in the cell for several days by the time I arrived. The conditions were, apparently, appalling – dark, cold and very dirty. He had been given only a small portion of food to eat once a day, and when I saw him he looked crushed. He was in such a bad state that he didn't even ask for my help, knowing as he did that it would be the end of his farm and the end of his livelihood. He was facing ruin.

The list of charges included the illegal use of electricity, concealing the evidence and killing the buffalo.

The best option I felt I had was to ask my relatives if they could help, as they were the only people who could have possibly known the police officers, or known some of their kin. I told them that I wanted to get Long out of that awful place. They said that it would probably cost about 5 million đồng to secure his release. He would also have to pay reparations to the owner, and this would be a further 500,000 đồng.

Fortunately I had brought enough money, so I asked my relative to arrange for his release as quickly as possible. The wait for Long's return was a painful one. I had no idea how he would be once freed, although I knew that the dreadful state of his new situation would weigh heavily on him. When he appeared at the door of my aunt's house the first thing he said was that I should return to Hà Nội immediately to be with my husband. He clearly felt guilty at having inconvenienced me, and Steve.

Long stayed in the area only long enough to sell his land, crop and hut. In total, he got 5 million đồng – a pittance considering the amount of effort he had put into building up the farm. He knew well that somebody who was not from that area and with a criminal record would be an easy target. He had no option but to leave.

Our new arrival

I was so happy when Leoni Yến Nhi was born. I was also happy with the way that Steve looked after us both. But when Leoni was just four months old our lives were turned upside down. By this time we had a helper in the house, a young woman called Xoài (Mango). She would look after Leoni if we were out at any time. One day, we were having lunch in a Thai restaurant when Steve said that he felt a bit unwell. His heartbeat was very irregular and he said that the safest thing to do would be to ride to the international hospital near to our home to get checked out. After a few nights in intensive care, the specialist said it would be best if Steve returned to his home country to get checked out thoroughly. There was really no option, so Steve asked the doctor to give him something to relax him for the journey ahead, which he would have to take by himself as Leoni didn't yet have a passport, and in any case was considered too young to fly. Steve was devastated at the prospect of having to return to the UK in this way. There was so little time and within just two days he had to fly home. Before he left he handed me a letter that he'd written in the hospital. He said that if anything should happen to him then I had to give the letter to his father. As he left us I could see tears in his eyes.

Over the next few weeks I had to focus on preparing to join him in the UK. This meant getting Leoni included on my passport, and arranging a visa for us both to travel to the UK. It also meant that I had to sell or give away all of our belongings, including the little car we had bought soon after Leoni was born to transport her around with us. This was a frantic time, especially because whoever had printed out my passport had given me the wrong name. This meant I had to return to my home district to get a special letter confirming that the two people on my passport and ID card were one and the same. Everything had to be translated and certified with a red stamp to give to the British Embassy. I was so fortunate because my uncle Tung was familiar with the visa process and he helped me. He also agreed to accompany me and Leoni to the UK. Knowing how travel sick I was, Steve had asked him to travel with us.

Before I set off to the UK I gave the letter Steve had given me to a friend, who spoke good English, to translate. When she told me what it said I was very emotional and burst into tears as it asked his father to help us if he wasn't lucky.

We arrived at Manchester Airport on a cold April day. Steve was there waiting with his father and he was clearly so relieved to see us again. He looked well, which was a relief. He said he was waiting for a check-up at a hospital in Liverpool, which was scheduled for a few days' time.

It had only been just over a year since I first visited Tony's house but such a lot had happened. And now I was here for the foreseeable future. Things seemed very different this time. Uncle Tung stayed for a few days, and then it was just the three of us. Steve's father kindly stayed at Aunt Berna's nearby house so that we could have his place to ourselves. The house was on a very quiet street and I struggled at first, used as I was to the hustle and bustle of Hà Nội. I remember being so happy when the bin men came along one day, and I waved to them in excitement – relieved that there was actually somebody on the street.

The weather was so cold and the skies seemed to be constantly grey. After the first month passed by I was feeling very homesick. I still spoke hardly any English and I missed Vietnamese food terribly. We were so busy arranging the basics of our new life that we didn't really have time to spend making ourselves comfortable.

Fortunately, Steve had good news from the hospital. Although he still had occasional irregular heartbeats they weren't considered to be life-threatening. It seemed that he could live a normal life. On hearing this news, Steve started to prepare for our next chapter. He said that we should move to a warmer part of the country, near to the seaside. He said that he had used to live in a small town in Kent and it would be a much better environment for us there.

Heading south

Because we wanted to leave as soon as possible, once we had bought a car we loaded up our few belongings and drove south. It was impossible to rent a house straight away, so Steve suggested that we went to a holiday caravan park to rent a caravan while we looked for a place, and also a job for him. I loved the caravan, which had everything we needed, and we spent a lot of time outside as the weather was much better.

Steve told me that it was proving impossible to rent a house until he had a job, so he had decided to contact the local newspaper group to see if there were any opportunities. He said that the money wouldn't be very good but at least we could get established and he would be nearby. The fact was we had used a large amount of our savings on the trip back to the UK and

Steve's hospital treatment in Việt Nam. Fortunately, the newspaper group agreed to take him on so he started work and we were able to rent a house.

We now had a small, terraced house in a seaside town on the north Kent coast. The house was in the town centre, which meant that all I had to do was walk a few hundred metres and I was on the main shopping street. This meant hustle and bustle. Other people.

The next few months were difficult. My homesickness had not gone away and life was really quite difficult. Steve's job paid him even less than he was expecting, so there was little money to do anything other than the basics. I did what I could to meet people while Steve was at work – joining a playgroup and taking Leoni to a baby group at the town library. Each day Steve would come home from work and he was always be happy to learn that I'd taken Leoni out and had made efforts to meet people. He said that I mustn't be too shy about not speaking English. Slowly I started to get to know more people, and very slowly my English started to improve. Everybody I met seemed friendly, and they always encouraged me to come along to different events.

I had brought a few books with me from Việt Nam to help me learn English and now I started to follow the lessons. I would learn a new word or two and look for opportunities to use them when I met people in the playgroup. I was so grateful that everybody I knew seemed to be helpful and encouraging.

After a few months in the house I was becoming more familiar with life in the West. I said to Steve that it was silly spending so much of our money on rent, when it was possible to borrow money from a bank and buy our own place. Steve did a few sums and said that we could probably afford a small house, using the deposit money his father had kindly offered to lend us. We started to look, and eventually found a three-bedroom place very near to where were renting. We needed a three-bedroom house because I had found out that I was pregnant again – with the baby due in June, 2001. We moved in to our new house and Steve started to redecorate in preparation for our new arrival.

Big sister arrives, and a new baby

Now we were really busy. With a new house and getting to know more people I had a lot of challenges in my life. This helped greatly with my homesickness. I had also started to think that I wanted my elder sister, Lien, to come over to the UK to help me with our new arrival. This meant a mountain of paperwork to prove to the government that we could support Lien while she was in the UK. It was quite a challenge but just before our baby was born, Lien arrived from Hà Nội. On our drive from Heathrow Airport, Steve asked Lien what her first impressions of England were and she replied that it was so green – crops would easily grow here.

Like me, she was a country girl at heart.

With Lien here I prepared for the birth, and was surprised when a few days earlier than expected my waters broke. It was 4am. In traditional Vietnamese culture women who have given birth are not allowed to wash their hair or shower for one month. Although I had no intention of sticking to this custom I had however decided to wait a few days before I washed my hair following the birth – so that meant I needed a shower and full hair wash now. I also needed to eat, so I boiled three eggs to give me energy and headed upstairs for a shower.

Only once finished did I call Steve, and told him that our new baby was coming. He thought I was joking, but I insisted that I had already prepared and was waiting to go. He looked shocked and asked if he had time to wash his face.

The seven-mile drive to the hospital was so painful with my contractions and I gripped the seat as hard as I could – demanding Steve slowed down, before demanding he speed up when the contractions had eased. Just as we approached the hospital blue flashing lights lit up the car and Steve said he had to stop. We'd been pulled over by the police for driving erratically. The police officer who approached the car looked horrified when she looked inside – and we had an blue-light escort for the rest of the journey.

When we arrived at the hospital I was ready. Knowing already how painful the process was going to be I decided that the best policy was speed. The midwife examined me and said I wasn't ready yet as dilation was only 5cm. She said she would return periodically to check on me. The contractions continued and during each one I pushed as hard as I could. Luckily, the midwife happened to put her head around the door during one contraction and couldn't believe the sight. Our baby was already halfway out and the midwife had to rush over to the bed to catch the rest of him.

At 4.1kg we had a healthy baby boy.

The midwife passed the baby, who we had decided to call Shea, to me but I was so exhausted I asked her to pass him to his proud dad, who exclaimed "hello mate". The nurse said I needed stitches but would have to wait a few hours for the doctor to arrive. When he examined me he said that I'd pushed too hard and now would need a lot of stitches. It would mean an overnight stay at hospital.

A new plan

The next day we returned home, and our new life began as a family of four. I soon realised that we needed extra income but had to wait until Shea was old enough to be looked after by Lien. After seven months I got a job at a local care home. The manager was very kind and we got on straight away. Despite my lack of English, the manager said she was very happy with the way I worked with other people and especially the residents. Even though my income was only small it meant that the money we had as a family increased a lot. It meant that we could start to consider things that we hadn't been able to. This included a trip to Việt Nam.

When I had left for the UK I had told my friends that I would be away for a maximum of five years. Although by now only three years had passed, both I and Steve were desperate to visit Việt Nam again. We had worked very hard trying to re-establish ourselves and were determined to realise our dream as quickly as possible. So we saved every penny we could and eventually had enough for a three-week trip.

The plane touched down, and in a short time we were once again in the teeming streets of Hà Nội. We wanted to be right at the heart of the city, so asked the taxi driver to head to the Hoàn Kiếm area. It was all I had been dreaming of for the last three years. People everywhere, traffic and noise. But now I was here my senses were completely swamped. The hustle and bustle I'd craved became a stifling crowd. The noise was too much. Worse, I felt like an idiot in this now unfamiliar environment so used had I become in such a relatively short time to life in England.

It didn't take us too long to adjust to things though, and when it was time to return to the UK we each acknowledged that we didn't really want to. So we agreed to a new plan: save money for the next year or so and then return to Việt Nam for a whole 12 months. With this plan, we were both happy – even in the knowledge that we had so much work to do before we could achieve it.

As soon as I returned I started working every shift that I could at the care home. Steve would return from work and immediately take me to the care home for a 12-hour night shift. In the morning I would return and Steve would head to work. I was working 70-hour weeks, while Steve was working extra at weekends whenever he could. We were so tired but the money towards our trip was quickly adding up.

Eventually we had enough for a year's travel in Việt Nam and we handed in our notices, and told Leoni's school that she would be away for a year. The plan was to travel the length of Việt Nam looking for a place to stay long-term and then put Leoni into a local school. She could already speak some Vietnamese and we thought that the adventure would be a good one for her, and for Shea.

The trip was so exciting. From working so hard right up until the day we left we now seemed to have all the time in the world. We travelled from Sài Gòn up to Hà Nội, staying wherever we liked. All the time our minds were buzzing with ideas. I realised that Steve had had enough of local journalism and he was starting to explore other options, while I knew that work was easy to find back in England and – in any case – there was lots of help available for families if they were ever struggling to find work. Coming from Việt Nam, with no such help, this was very reassuring.

When we reached Hội An we thought that it was an ideal place to stay – a lovely, gentle ancient town with historic sites and wonderful food. Ideal for children – and adults. We quickly settled into a routine – finding a few restaurants we liked and a house to rent. We also found a school willing to take Leoni and enrolled her into it.

By now our minds were really zooming through ideas of what we could do when we returned. There seemed to be so many options. Eventually we settled on a simple one: to import a variety of things from Việt Nam to market in the UK when we returned. Like the fishermen in the Hội An river we cast a wide net, buying all kinds of bits – some large, some small – to ship back to England. As a tourist hub Hội An seemed to have everything Việt Nam had to offer – from cheap caps and T-shirts to beautiful silk bags and lanterns. We even found a superb joiner along the river who we commissioned to make silk-panelled hardwood room screens. We slowly collected things to ship back to the UK so that, once home, another new chapter could start.

Things weren't always easy in Hội An. The school experience for poor Leoni had been terrible as the only foreign child there and Steve decided to remove her from it and teach her himself. He also did the same for Shea, although he stayed enrolled at the local nursery for mornings. Leoni joined him so that the two of them could be together. So we were now home-schooling Leoni and Shea for a few hours each day, and had lots of adventures through it. Steve saw it as an opportunity to educate the children in a more natural way – to use the things we did each day as part of the lessons. We ended up making video clips and even a newspaper page of life in this old town.

On the road again

After a final month in Hà Nội we assembled all of the things we had bought and arranged for them to be shipped back, while we flew back. Now we had a new challenge: where to sell the things that we'd bought. At first we started small – at local town fairs, before getting a bit more ambitious and booking some festivals. It quickly became clear that the people who liked our stock tended to be older, and Steve decided that folk festivals would be the best place to sell our stuff.

Things quickly mushroomed and before long we were making more money than we ever had before. The festivals were extremely hard work as initially we were living out of a tent and having to look after Leoni and Shea while tending the stall. Hours were long at these events and some – especially Glastonbury – were noisy throughout the night. We rarely slept well, although things improved when, by chance, we spotted an old caravan for sale close to our home. What luxury this old thing represented compared with our humble tent.

As we became busier with this new business, the children had to spend more and more time away from school. Fortunately, the head teacher at the children's school was very understanding – knowing that Steve was filling in any gaps in their education while we were away.

After four years of this I began to think that although we had quite a good life the job was unsustainable in the long-term. I decided to follow what so many other Vietnamese did and learn to be a nail technician. As well as helping to run our festival business, Steve had already started to edit books and could work from anywhere. I quickly found a trainee position at my local nail bar and, after six months of training, got a job there.

Three years later and I had my own salon, in a little historic Kent town, where we had already bought a holiday-let house. For the next ten years I ran the shop, and was happy there until one day I started to develop an allergy to something I was using. This got progressively worse and made my eyes stream with water and become itchy in the extreme. Now I would finish my shift at the salon and have to sit at home with my eyes closed in constant pain. Steve said I had to stop and, reluctantly, I had to agree with him.

So now another chapter has begun. I now have time to enjoy life and do the things I want to do. I feel so lucky to have my family and Steve as my husband. All he ever wants is for his family to be happy and he cares for us so well. I cherish this and the fact that he is in my life. I feel such good fortune, and feel it is the same for our children. I'm thankful for my family and for the opportunity I've been given to live in an environment where

I've been able to change – to learn a different way of life in such a civilised society.

Without the encouragement of my husband and our children I would never have dared to so confidently write down my feelings, and some of the experiences I've had. I now have a richness in my life that has allowed me to capture some of these moments, these life events. It is a richness that had been denied me when I was young. I hope only that in reading this somebody else who had been similarly denied will find a voice to write their own story, and in-so-doing come to terms with things that have happened to them, as I have done by writing this.

So where does this leave my story? Much of the above happened a long time ago now – back when Việt Nam was still a very poor country, full of poor people with few prospects of improving their lives. And what of little Luyến, my baby sister? I still have no idea where she is or of what happened to her. She is so often in my thoughts though as the final piece in our family story that still has no place. But when I reflect on the kind of life she may have had I know at least that she has almost certainly had a better life than she would have had with my father. As a baby she would probably have gone to a family who needed a daughter, and been brought up as such. Not as a maid like me but hopefully as a full member of a family, albeit very likely a poor one. She could have lived in a loving home, and herself be a loving mother now – with no knowledge of me, so far away, wondering what became of her.

A letter to my brother, Long

My brother. Are you okay, truly? When I think about you it's all I want to know. I always feel pride that you are my brother. You always made me feel secure when I was little – I knew that I couldn't be bullied when you were around. Now, even at 48 years of age, I still have that feeling when I think of you. You were so talented when we were children – the best in the village at catching fish, eels crabs, snails – anything that moved and could be eaten. Every day you were the one who always went out to catch food. You kept us going with things to sell at market – and things to keep father happy when he drank his rice wine. Whatever the season, you were the best at foraging. Your hands were never empty. The older I got the more I understood that you had no choice in this. All of our lives were so hard, but yours was the most brutal. We were younger and we relied on you. When you are as hungry as we were you have no energy. But it didn't stop our father's demands. We had only fear left – of hunger and of random beatings. Too many beatings, especially for you. There was always a cane ready to whip you with. How many times did we all have to lie on the floor as father stood over us lashing us with his cane? How many times did we have to stand against the wall, our arms outstretched as he did the same? I can still feel the terrible stings of that cane, and see the swellings that would so blight our arms, hands, legs and backs. I was the lucky one. I was younger and was hit less than you. I learned to scream the loudest whereas you bit your lip and took the pain. When father had finished he would tell us all to go away – and to make sure that we didn't catch his eye. No crying was allowed. If we did, the beatings would continue.

I remember all those mornings that you had to get up at 4.30am to boil the kettle for father before starting your studies. I remember us huddled around the little kerosene lamp waiting for dawn to break. Father would sit next to you to check you were doing your homework. I can remember all the slaps to your face and head if you misread a word, and father's shouts of "ngu. Ngu!" (stupid. Stupid!). I could feel your fear as father grabbed your hair and banged your head against the wall. It made you struggle with the words even more. I know that because of all the work you had to do you had to miss too much school, and this made your struggle all the more difficult.

I can remember father teaching me how to make letters, using a stick on our dirt floor, and him telling me to make the shape of an egg for the letter 'o', and then to add the different tone marks like the dấu mũ (hat). But we only got as far as the letter 'o' and three tone marks. That was the extent of my education. Like you I was called stupid if he tested me and I made a mistake. But you always got the worst of it.

I was lucky because I escaped from this ignorance, and discovered a different world. When I returned I found only you living at home with father. We were both so much more mature and we had changed so greatly. I noticed that the thin cane that used to whip us had been replaced by a large bamboo pole. The torture was only worse but I couldn't show you any pity when father was beating you in case he started to beat me, too. One time I thought father had killed you when he struck you on the head with a brick. You disappeared for the whole day and night after that. I was so scared. Then somebody told me you had climbed a tree at the end of the village and was hiding there. Father was so angry that he locked the front door and wired the back door to our hut so that you would get an electric shock when you touched it. I couldn't sleep that night – desperate to hear you coming home so that I could stop you from touching the door. I was so happy that I was awake when you returned and could let you in the front door. The next day I told you about what father had done. You said you already knew. Maybe father had done it before and I hadn't known about it.

Do you remember me telling you about Hà Nội and where I was staying the first time I returned? About what my life was like? You listened to me and said that your dream was to one day have enough money to visit Hà Nội, at least once. I asked you then if you could take me back with you. I really wanted us both to go, in the hope that you would run away as well. But you only said maybe. I also thought about Lien – perhaps she would go with me.

The day I ran away to find Lien I had to leave you. I knew what I was leaving you to and my tears flowed as the wheels of the coach turned. As I disappeared down the road my hurt was so great. I couldn't control my tears because I knew the torture you would be receiving as father demanded to know where I was. All I could do was to close my eyes and hope for a miracle that somebody, something would pick you up and sit you next to me on the coach and we would drive off together.

Was it five, six or seven years later when we next met? You hadn't been home when I returned with Lien and father had disowned us. I had returned home and told you that I could show you around Hà Nội if you ever visited. And then one day you came. You had finally made it to Hà Nội. That journey of just 40km may as well have been 1,000km. Do you remember me asking if you liked it? Do you remember me telling you that at last it wasn't a dream anymore – it was a reality?

Dear brother, now I'm sure you have so much experience of life, on the road you have taken. The truth is I know it has not been easy. Isn't that correct? But I understand one thing – that our hearts beat as one and this unity will surely draw our blood to flow together wherever we are. I know that you have had your dreams over the years, and have chased many opportunities when they presented themselves. You have worked so hard, with dedication and loyalty, but the result is still zero. Your life has been so tough and the disappointment you must feel is crushing. I am the one who has witnessed this, standing at your side even when we are so far apart. Remember when I asked you again what was your dream? You told me that you wanted a job with a salary, and that when you had some money the first thing you would do is to help our youngest sisters, Ly and Liễu, to go to school until they didn't want to learn anymore. The second thing you would do was to save money so that father could be cremated when he died and have a proper funeral. You said that this would cost 30 million đồng. These were your goals.

I don't want to talk any more about the suffering of the past. It makes me feel so bitter. I only want you to try and create the conditions in your life that will give those who care about you the opportunity to be closer to you, to live as true sisters and brother. Please remember to try and forget the past, and instead live life as somebody with wisdom who can forgive, and in-so-doing breathe new life where so much pain used to exist.

I am your loving sister and I will always be at your side.

Lan

A letter to my father

Father, allow me to say something of what I see, hear and know of you. I would like to start by asking whether your life is a lonely one? There is a mountain of stories that brought you to this lonely place.

I want to ask: were you your own enemy, or were your enemies your wife and your children?

I guess you were happy once, when my mother was alive. I heard when I was older that mum had died of an electric shock. I was no more than three at the time. You were left with three young children. I'm sure that was difficult. That is why somebody helped you, by introducing you to a woman who could become your second wife. You married and we had a stepmother. Now there was help to manage our fields and the daily chores. Did happiness visit you again? I guess it did, for you had three more children.

Many people said that you were talented and highly educated. It can be true that living with highly educated people is not always easy. The home that you created for this life was just a simple hut with a straw roof. In it were locked six children and a wife. Our joy was the good name our family had because of your education. People say it is difficult to lose wisdom, and wise people can quickly adapt to situations when there are difficulties to face. But it seems to me that this doesn't fit our family situation with you in charge.

I don't want to talk about life too much because it is too difficult. But please, on this occasion, listen to how I feel about you.

Your real talent was to terrify people. You always gave us orders, but never instructions. You ordered us to cook, but there was no food to prepare. We had to go and find it. All you gave us were demands. You just sat and drank your wine and barked orders. All you did was beat us if we didn't please you. You treated us like animals, and told us that the pigs were more intelligent than we were. You said that even the dogs had a use, unlike us. You would lie to us, accusing us of doing things we hadn't done.

But you didn't stop there. You would accuse other people of taking things from you, and demand that they paid you even when they had done nothing wrong. You did this so carefully – not by shouting, but by cold words when they were vulnerable. You knew exactly what you were doing, and how to manipulate people. As time went on this beast inside you got bigger and bigger, until eventually through fear even your wife and children had to join this slandering of others.

But this wasn't the worst thing you ever did that I have seen with my own eyes. Do you remember when I was six or seven years old and you accused Mợ Hà of doing terrible things? You had been drinking rice wine and you were shouting so much. You said that so much unhusked rice had gone missing and you accused her of selling it and sending the money to her family. You tortured her, but she denied doing anything. But you didn't stop and you just carried on beating her. You stripped her, tied her hands and feet together and kicked her and hit her until all her body was black and blue. Do you remember how you did this all day and all night too until in the end she said that Lien had done it? She said that just so the beatings would stop.

So then you started beating Liên, but she denied she had done anything. Lien said she hadn't seen anybody doing anything, and in any case she was too small to carry the 30kg or 40kg you said had gone missing.

For a whole day and night Mợ Hà was tied up, with no food or drink. By the evening of the next night she begged for something to eat, and you said that she was allowed to eat only excrement. Do you remember that you called me and Lien over and we stood in front of your kerosene lamp. We looked down and saw the fear in Mợ Hà's eyes. You told us to go to the cesspit in the corner of the garden with a bowl and to fill that bowl with excrement. You gave the bowl to Lien and passed me the lamp. We were so scared. But when we got there it was just too terrible a thing to do, so we waited, scared that he kerosene lamp would run out of fuel. We crept back and stood by the back door, but you heard us and you shouted for us to bring in the bowl. We said that there was nothing to collect. But you just demanded we return with what he wanted, and warned us that if we didn't he would take us there, grab our hair and force our heads into the pit. So we had to return.

This time I had the bowl and Lien had the lamp. But when I looked at the pit I said to Lien that we still couldn't do it. We were so terrified of what you would do that do you know what I did? I took my pants down and squeezed out a poo into the bowl. My young mind thought that at least this would be fresh, so I was doing my stepmother a favour. This time when we returned we handed you the bowl – once you'd unlocked the door. When you took the bowl you told us to go out. But you hadn't realised that we were watching through a hole in the wall. We watched as you took the ties off Mợ Hà's hands and left the bowl near her still-tied feet. You told her to eat with her bare hands – and said that only when she had eaten the whole bowl would she be released. We watched as Mợ Hà tried to eat. But she just vomited – and you shouted at her that if she vomited any more she would have to eat that as well.

Our poor stepmother – your wife – started to eat. I don't know how long it took but we could watch no more. After it was all over and you had untied her feet Mợ Hà walked quietly past us and jumped into the pond at the end of the garden to try and wash herself. Nothing was ever said of this.

As time went on we gradually started to leave you. Your family was disappearing from your life. Even the animals died through neglect. We each found our own ways to escape your evil.

I'm sure you're not happy reading these words. But I want you to know that I have held these thoughts inside me for so long that I could bear it no longer. Now, I have released them.

You need to know one thing, father: I am scared of you no more.

Your daughter Lan

Epilogue

In 2023 I returned with my family to Hà Nội. I took my husband and children to the area that used to be my home – the network of alleyways, the station, and the public toilet, where the tap and the rubbish tip that had once sustained us used to be. Along with the rubbish tip, the tap is long since gone, and the public toilets are now much improved. The area is still a bit scruffy – with none of the smart cafes or shops like in many other areas of Hà Nội.

While there I heard a passing man call out "Lan". I turned and recognised him straight away as being the elder brother of Thuy, who had been one of my close friends at the time. She had been adopted by another family, after being abandoned in the same public toilets by her birth mother. She also sold food through the night as a child.

I arranged to meet Thủy in a city-centre café, where we spent an hour or two reminiscing, talking of a life long gone. And on my way out, Thủy stopped me and said that of all the people we knew at that time only two had managed to truly escape their previous lives. One was me, and the other was the đầu gấu who ran the station with such an iron fist. He is now a wealthy man, with several houses and a legitimate business. For the rest, it's still dust.

Acknowledgements

It took me a long time to even decide to write this book, and many times I thought I would abandon it. But several people close to me persuaded me to continue, and helped me to edit and proofread my work. I want to thank Leoni and Shea for their encouragement, and especially Steve for his help with all stages of my work. Without his help this book would not have happened.

I would also like to thank all the friends who have given me the confidence to continue, and anybody who has taken the time to read my story.

The author, Lan Anh Hoàng, in 2024

Printed in Great Britain
by Amazon